DIP IN

First published in Great Britain in 2025 by Hamlyn, an imprint of Octopus Publishing Group Ltd
Carmelite House
50 Victoria Embankment
London EC4Y 0DZ
www.octopusbooks.co.uk
www.octopusbooksusa.com

An Hachette UK Company
www.hachette.co.uk

The authorized representative in the EEA is Hachette Ireland, 8 Castlecourt Centre, Dublin 15, D15 XTP3, Ireland (info@hbgi.ie)

Distributed in the US by Hachette Book Group, 1290 Avenue of the Americas, 4th and 5th Floors, New York, NY 10104

Distributed in Canada by Canadian Manda Group, 664 Annette St., Toronto, Ontario, Canada M6S 2C8

ISBN 978-1-80419-272-6

A CIP catalogue record for this book is available from the British Library.

Printed and bound in China.

10 9 8 7 6 5 4 3 2 1

Junior Commissioning Editors:
Samhita Foria and Isabel Jessop
Editor: Scarlet Furness
Art Director: Yasia Williams
Designer: Emma Wells, Studio Nic+Lou
Copy Editor: Tara O'Sullivan
Food Stylist: Sonali Shah
Assistant Food Stylists:
Kristine Jakobsson and Lucy Cottle
Props Stylist: Max Robinson
Photographer: Cara Cormack
Senior Production Manager: Peter Hunt

Standard level spoon measurements are used in all recipes.
1 tablespoon = one 15 ml spoon
1 teaspoon = one 5 ml spoon

Both imperial and metric measurements have been given in all recipes. Use one set of measurements only and not a mixture of both.

Eggs should be medium unless otherwise stated. The Department of Health advises that eggs should not be consumed raw. This book contains dishes made with raw or lightly cooked eggs. It is prudent for more vulnerable people such as pregnant and nursing mothers, the elderly, babies and young children to avoid uncooked or lightly cooked dishes made with eggs. Once prepared these dishes should be kept refrigerated and used promptly.

Milk should be full fat unless otherwise stated.

Fresh herbs should be used unless otherwise stated. If unavailable use dried herbs as an alternative but halve the quantities stated.

Ovens should be preheated to the specific temperature – if using a fan-assisted oven, follow manufacturer's instructions for adjusting the time and the temperature.

This book includes dishes made with nuts and nut derivatives. It is advisable for those with known allergic reactions to nuts and nut derivatives and those who may be potentially vulnerable to these allergies, such as pregnant and nursing mothers, the elderly, babies and children, to avoid dishes made with nuts and nut oils. It is also prudent to check the labels of pre-prepared ingredients for the possible inclusion of nut derivatives.

Vegetarians should look for the 'V' symbol on a cheese to ensure it is made with vegetarian rennet.

FSC
www.fsc.org
MIX
Paper | Supporting responsible forestry
FSC® C008047

DIP IN

80 DELICIOUS DIP RECIPES FOR ENTERTAINING, SNACKING & BEYOND

SONALI SHAH

hamlyn

Contents

It's Time to Dip In!

Need an easy contribution for a picnic with friends? Dip it.

Want stunning small plates for impressive entertaining? Dip it.

Craving a quick and delicious snack to tide you over until dinner? Dip it. Dip it real good.

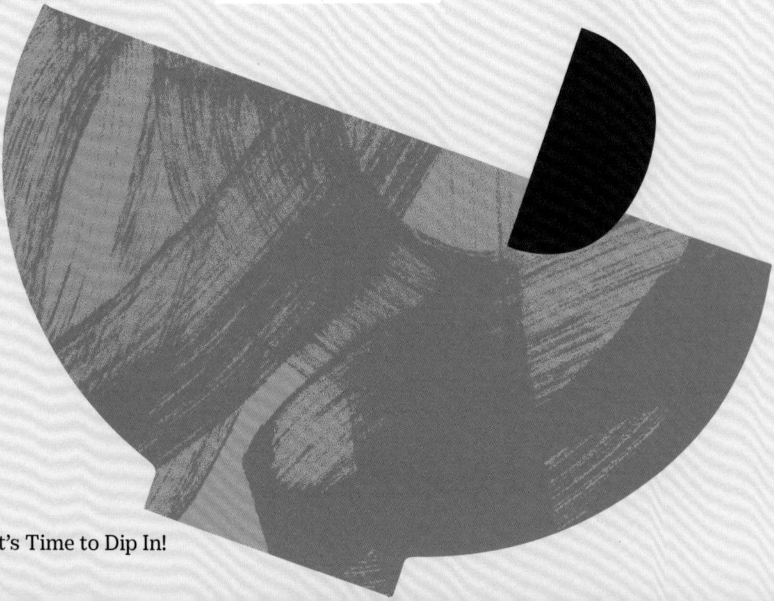

There is no mood or occasion that can't be improved by a dip, and *Dip In* is here to show you how to truly make the most of this scrumptious and versatile dish. A delicious dip can be made using affordable ingredients and store cupboard staples. Blend some avocados with fresh herbs, jalapeños and limes and suddenly you've an Avocado Green Goddess Dip (see page 41). Raid your refrigerator for feta, yogurt and tomatoes, whiz up Whipped Feta & Burned Tomatoes with Ginger & Spring Onion Dressing (see page 104) and you're in dipping heaven.

If you're looking for a way to use up a trickier ingredient, dips are also the answer. The sumac hidden at the back of the cupboard? Impress your guests with a sizzling Date & Sumac Baked Camembert (see page 113). A jar of miso you bought for one recipe and never used again? Whip up some Miso Mushroom & Whisky Pâté (see page 95).

The internationally recognized beauty of dips is affirmed by their presence in cultures and cuisines around the world. Of course, there are the classics: salsa and guacamole from Mexico, or baba ganoush and hummus from the Middle East. But think also of pesto from Italy, ezme from Turkey, romesco from Spain, tzatziki from Greece, zaalouk from Morocco, gzik from Poland, anchoïade from France, chimichurri from Argentina, nam pla prik from Thailand...the list goes on. From Rome to Bangkok, we love to dip!

The recipes in this book take influence and inspiration from dips around the world. They offer easy and exciting ways to experiment with flavours and ingredients that you may not have encountered before. Dips are a fun and low-stakes way to try something different or add an exciting new flavour boost to a dish you already love.

Now, it's all very well to celebrate the virtues and delights of dips, but what exactly constitutes a dip? Where is the line crossed into sauces, dressings, mousses, relishes and chutneys? Where does the nebulous concept of 'condiment' come into all this? Well, as far as this book goes, as long as your dish can be eaten by dunking something else into it, then you're in dipping territory. The dips range from smooth to chunky, from sweet to savoury. They can be eaten hot or cold, as a main or a dessert. Whether you're looking for something spicy or refreshing, nutty or herby, syrupy or tart, dips can have it all. Follow your instincts – if you can dip it, it's a dip.

The chapters that follow are curated to match you to your perfect dip, whatever the occasion. **In a Dash** contains dips that can all be made in 15 minutes or less, for a super-quick dip fix. **Graze** has dips that are perfect for sharing, as part of a picnic, buffet or grazing board. **Feast** is for your dinner party moments, and **Impress** is packed with dips designed to wow. **Meals** are dips that can be enjoyed as a whole meal and, last but certainly not least, **Desserts** has your sweet dip hits!

Now you may be wondering what you should be using to dunk, scoop and dip into all this deliciousness... Just turn to page 12 for your dip-spiration!

DIP TIP: SERVING SIZES

The serving sizes given in this book are only approximate. How far a dip will stretch depends on many factors, including what it's being served with, whether it's being used as a snack, side dish or showpiece, and your own appetite! For recipes in In a Dash, Graze, Feast and Impress, the suggested serving sizes are given for the dips as a side dish, or part of a larger spread. On the other hand, the recipes in Meals and Desserts are designed to be enjoyed as a full main meal or dessert portion respectively, so this is reflected in the serving sizes.

DIP TIP: KEEPING YOUR DIPS

Most of the dips will last for one to two days after you've made them, so just pop them in a sealed container in the refrigerator if you'd like to make them in advance or enjoy some tasty leftovers.

DIP TIP: KEY EQUIPMENT

Many of the dips in this book can be made with standard kitchen equipment, with knives, graters, whisks, mashers and mixing spoons being used to bring your dips together. However, others do require a blender or food processor to achieve the right consistency. Some of these you may be able to adapt if you're happy with a chunkier texture – for example, chopping ingredients finely or using a pestle and mortar instead. Feel free to experiment and adjust to suit your own kitchen, needs and vision – a dash of creativity could be the making of a fantastic new dip!

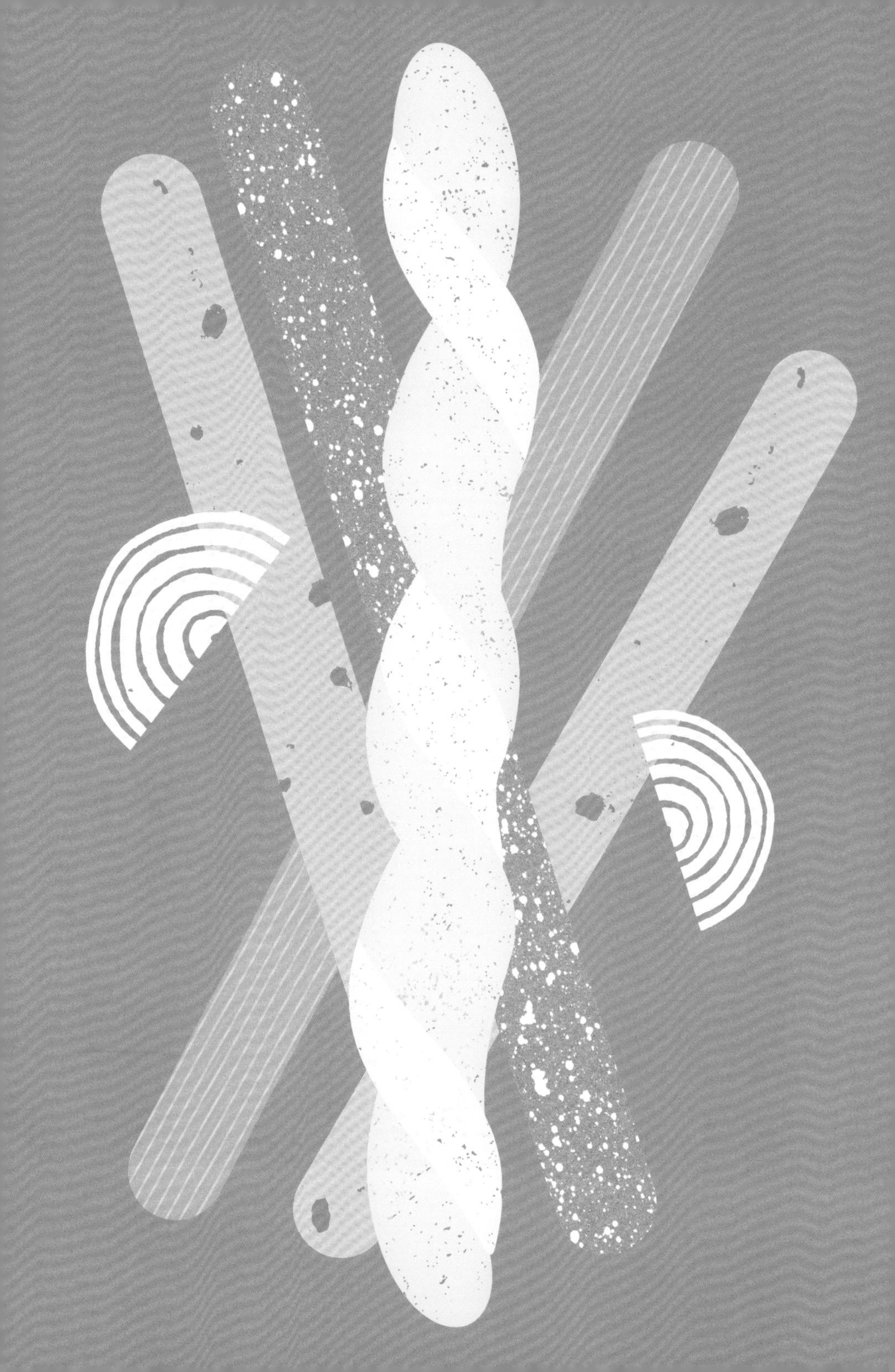

Dipper Party Menus

A selection of dips and dippers makes wonderful party food – whether it's for a sit-down dinner, a potluck, a buffet, a picnic or a party. By picking and choosing from across the different chapters in this book, you can easily create your own sensational spread, but here are a few thematic selections to get your dipper party planning started!

A MIDDLE EASTERN FEAST

Celebrate Middle Eastern flavours with a rich and creamy Courgette Mutabal (see page 49), refreshing Mast O Khiar (see page 21) and an upgrade on classic hummus with a Black Chickpea Hummus Bil Lahme (see page 142). For your dippers, try soft and fluffy flatbreads, smoky grilled vegetables and perhaps some grilled meat skewers. For dessert, finish with Firni with Rose & Pistachio (see page 154).

AN INDIAN-INSPIRED BANQUET

Indian dips are great served alongside a curry, but can also make a filling and flavour-packed meal on their own. The Seven-Layer Chaat Dip (see page 120) makes a stunning centrepiece. The Spinach & Mint Raita (see page 83) is cool and refreshing, while Coriander Chutney (see page 22) brings a bit of heat. Naan breads and poppadoms make the perfect accompanying dippers. You can finish with Shrikhand Parfait with Saffron Peaches & Almond Brittle for dessert (see page 163).

GLOWING GREEN VEGAN SPREAD

Celebrate zesty, herby plant-based food with this zingy collection of green dips: Rocket, Jalapeño & Cashew Pesto (see page 18), Avocado Green Goddess Dip (see page 41), Green Mojo (see page 61) and Creamy Edamame & Wasabi Dip (see page 86). Take the celebration of all things green further by serving the spread with your favourite veg: cucumber, mangetout, asparagus and more.

TAPAS TIME!

Spain is famous for its sharing tapas dishes, so it makes perfect sense to share some fiery Spanish-inspired dips with friends. Try serving Spinach & 'Nduja Cannellini Beans (see page 146) with a Salsa Romesco (see page 46), Spicy Garlic & Sun-Dried Tomato Prawns (see page 141) and Ajo Blanco with Spicy Paprika Pulled Mushrooms (see page 84). Complete your Spanish spread with some crackers, Padron peppers, olives and Piri Piri Aioli (see page 38). All delicious served with a crisp cold beer!

BRUNCHY DIPS

It's time for brunch to get a dippable upgrade. Lay out Everything-but-the-Bagel Dip (see page 74), Bloody Maria Prawn Cocktail Dip (see page 109) and Poached Eggs with Tadka Butter (see page 135), add some bagel chips and crusty bread, get your pals over and dip in.

BARBECUE

Nourishing, summery dips make the perfect accompaniment to a barbecue. Serve a hearty Japanese-Style Potato Salad (see page 69), crunchy Esquites (see page 60) and Coconut & Spiced Black Bean Dip with Pineapple Salsa (see page 90) for a splash of sunshine alongside your barbecued vegetables or meats. Or enjoy with some tortilla chips for snacking while the barbecue heats up!

What Do I Dip With?

You can enjoy the dips in this book with anything you like! But while I've suggested some of my favourite dippers throughout the recipes, I encourage you to be creative and mix and match with what you have to hand. If you're serving the dips as part of a table spread, it's good to have a selection. Here are some of my favourites.

BAGEL CHIPS
These are similar to crostini (see opposite), but you make them with bagels. Carefully slice some bagels into thin rounds, then place in a single layer on a baking sheet, drizzling over some oil and seasoning. Bake in a preheated oven, 200°C/180°C fan (400°F), Gas Mark 6, for 10–12 minutes, turning halfway, or until crispy. You can always substitute bagel chips with crostini if you don't have time to make these.

BREAD
Bread is always a classic go-to for dips, and luckily we have hundreds of varieties out there! I would say let the cuisine lead you, but there are no hard-and-fast rules here. You want a variety of textures on the table, so a mixture of softer breads and crunchy breads is what I normally like. International supermarkets always have a good range of breads (some even have bakeries within them), and this is where I normally buy my naans, flatbreads and Turkish breads. If you have any Italian delis near you, these are great places to grab focaccia and ciabatta.

BREADSTICKS
Breadsticks are a good vessel for when you have a buffet table or garden party, as your guests can grab and go. Choose ones that work well with the flavour profiles of your chosen dips.

CRACKERS
Crackers are not just for Christmas! They're great whether you're creating a grazing board or table (with a few dips, of course!) or a buffet table. If you're choosing crackers for dinner parties, go for more premium brands or styles. You can also get rice crackers and prawn crackers from Asian supermarkets.

CRISPBREADS
Crispbreads originated in Scandinavia, but luckily these can be found in many supermarkets globally now. They're great as they keep for a while in your cupboard, and come in a variety of flavours, like sesame, seeded and rye. You can either use them to scoop the dips, or spread the dips on top and add other toppings to make a quick and delicious snack.

CROSTINI
Crostini are mini Italian toasts traditionally made from ciabatta. You can buy them ready-made, but sometimes you open a bag and half of them are crushed, which is quite annoying if you're planning on serving a platter of dip-topped crostini to your guests. Luckily, they're really easy to make! Follow the same recipe for making bagel chips (see opposite), but use sliced ciabatta (or baguettes) instead.

CRUDITÉS
This is just a general term for fresh vegetables that you can use for dipping. Most commonly, these are things like sliced cucumbers, carrots or celery, but you can always experiment a bit further. Why not use sugar snap peas, radishes, endives and baby peppers? I also love to quickly blanch Tenderstem broccoli, asparagus and green beans, then plunge them into a bowl of iced water to keep them green. These make a great addition to my crudité boards. The more colourful, the better!

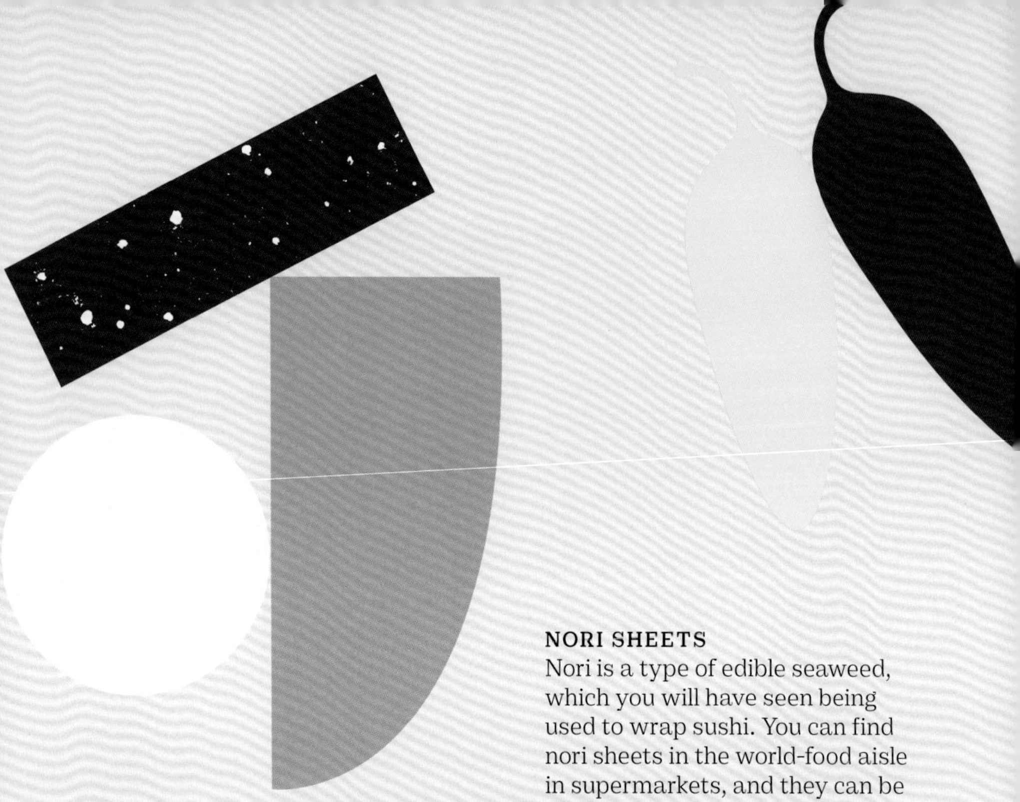

GRILLED VEGETABLES
Lightly oil and season vegetables like sliced aubergines, courgettes, peppers and spring onions, before adding them to a hot griddle (or frying) pan or to your barbecue. Other veg that also work well are cauliflower, broccoli and shallots.

LETTUCE OR ENDIVE CUPS
These work well for scooping, but also where the dip would complement a fresh and crunchy accompaniment.

NORI SHEETS
Nori is a type of edible seaweed, which you will have seen being used to wrap sushi. You can find nori sheets in the world-food aisle in supermarkets, and they can be eaten raw alongside Japanese-style dishes. I often cut them into small pieces and add them to my table for guests to use as a vessel to enjoy raw fish like salmon and tuna. They're also great served with prawn dips.

PADRON PEPPERS
Padron peppers are best charred in a hot, dry frying pan for a couple of minutes or until charred all over. You then drizzle them with olive oil and sprinkle over lots of sea salt.

PITTA CHIPS
Pitta chips are simply crisps made from stale pittas (you can buy pittas in most supermarkets). I like to eat them with more Mediterranean-style dips, but they have quite a neutral flavour so

work with other cuisines too. You can easily make them by tearing up some leftover pittas into small pieces, placing on a baking sheet with a little olive oil, and baking them in a preheated oven, 200°C/180°C fan (400°F), Gas Mark 6, for 10–12 minutes or until super crispy, turning regularly so they cook evenly.

POPPADOMS

I suggest eating these with South Asian-inspired dips, but as they have quite a neutral flavour, they'd work well with most dips.

POTATO CRISPS

Potato crisps are the easiest thing to put out for a party or gathering. I prefer using crunchy ridged ones for dips, but you can grab whatever you like – just try to make sure the flavour complements your dip; you don't want competing flavours.

SHISO LEAVES

Shiso (sometimes known as perilla) is a peppery leaf with a slightly citrus taste, found in Japanese and Korean cuisines. It's often eaten with sushi or as part of a Korean barbecue table, and can be easily found in Japanese/Korean grocery stores or online.

TORTILLA CHIPS

Tortilla chips are what you would normally use to make nachos, and you can get a variety of brands and flavours from all supermarkets.

A SPOON!

Always an option! Sometimes you just want to dip straight in!

In a Dash

This chapter is all about speed – for when you've got last-minute guests coming over or you're invited to a party but don't have much time to prep anything. Each dip can be made in under 15 minutes. Enjoy these speedy recipes with your favourite breads, crackers, potato crisps or crudités.

Rocket, Jalapeño & Cashew Pesto

With no chopping, this dip couldn't be easier! A little twist on the usual pesto, the creaminess from the cashews balancing nicely with the spicy jalapeños.

• SERVES 2–3

15 g (½ oz) sliced jalapeños from a jar, plus 1 tablespoon brine
25 g (1 oz) cashew nuts
40 g (1½ oz) rocket
4 tablespoons extra virgin olive oil
salt and freshly ground black pepper

• METHOD

Combine the jalapeños and brine, cashew nuts and rocket in a food processor. Season with a pinch of black pepper and blitz until chunky.

Add the olive oil and blend for a further 5–10 seconds, or until smooth and well combined. Taste for seasoning, adding a little salt if required, then serve.

DIPPING SUGGESTION
Crusty bread.

Mast O Khiar

This famous Persian yogurt is one of my absolute favourite dips. The sweetness from the sultanas works so well with the cooling cucumber and crunchy walnuts.

- **SERVES 2**

100 g (3½ oz) cucumber, grated
1 teaspoon salt
25 g (1 oz) sultanas
200 ml (7 fl oz) Greek yogurt
1 teaspoon dried mint
30 g (1 oz) walnuts, roughly chopped
15 g (½ oz) dill, roughly chopped, plus a few fronds to garnish
olive oil, for drizzling

- **METHOD**

Tip the grated cucumber into a sieve over a bowl and sprinkle with the salt. Add the sultanas to a separate bowl and pour over enough boiling water to cover. Leave both for 10 minutes – the salt will draw out moisture from the cucumber and the sultanas will plump up.

Meanwhile, add the Greek yogurt to a mixing bowl with the mint and half the chopped walnuts. Stir to combine.

Once the cucumber has been draining for 10 minutes, squeeze to remove any extra liquid, then add the cucumber to the yogurt. Drain the sultanas and add half to the mixing bowl along with the chopped dill. Stir well to combine and taste for seasoning, adjusting by adding more salt if needed.

Transfer the dip into a serving bowl. Drizzle over some olive oil and garnish with the remaining chopped walnuts, sultanas and dill fronds.

DIPPING SUGGESTION
It's great with flatbreads, but also wonderful as part of a large meal with grilled meats like chicken wings or lamb chops, kebabs (meat or veggie) and rice.

Coriander Chutney

A good coriander chutney is so important to have in your cooking arsenal. Not only can you eat it by itself, you can also add it to yogurt to make an easy coriander yogurt, or use it as a marinade. You can adjust the spice level here, so feel free to increase the chillies if you like the heat.

- **SERVES 2–3**

large handful mint leaves
40 g (1½ oz) fresh coriander, leaves and stalks roughly chopped
2–3 green chillies, roughly chopped
2.5 cm (1 inch) piece of fresh root ginger, peeled and roughly chopped
2 teaspoons lemon juice
pinch of granulated sugar
salt

- **METHOD**

Add the mint, coriander, chillies and ginger to a food processor and blend until you have a paste.

Add the lemon juice, sugar and a pinch of salt, along with a splash of water, and blend again until well combined. You might need to add another splash of water to get it to a dipping consistency.

DIPPING SUGGESTION
This is delicious with samosas and pakoras, but it's equally good with really crunchy fries!

Mombasa Coconut Chutney

My mum's been making this dip for as long as I can remember, and it's very common in Kenyan Indian households, as it has its origins in Mombasa. It couldn't be easier.

- SERVES 2–3

100 g (3½ oz) desiccated coconut
20 g (¾ oz) fresh coriander, leaves and stalks finely chopped
2–3 green chillies, finely chopped
250 ml (8 fl oz) natural yogurt
pinch of granulated sugar
salt

- METHOD

Simply add everything to a bowl and mix until combined, seasoning with a pinch of salt.

DIPPING SUGGESTION
I love eating this with crispy bhajia *(pakoras).*

Tahini, Honey & Harissa Burned Butter

A deliciously salty, sweet and spicy butter with the nutty flavour of tahini.

- SERVES 3–4

100 g (3½ oz) salted butter
2 teaspoons black sesame seeds
1 tablespoon tahini
1 teaspoon honey
½ teaspoon harissa

- METHOD

Place a heatproof bowl into the refrigerator for 10–15 minutes or until cold.

Melt the butter in a small nonstick saucepan over a medium heat for 5–6 minutes until it has browned to a dark biscuit colour. Remove from the heat once browned and add the black sesame seeds – this is your 'burned butter'.

Add the butter to the cold mixing bowl, then stir in the tahini, honey and harissa. Leave aside to firm up slightly (chill in the refrigerator for 5 minutes if required), then use a small whisk to whip until fluffy.

DIPPING SUGGESTION
Really good crusty bread.

Ezme

This is the spicy red sauce that comes to the table with fluffy bread at most Turkish restaurants. It's also great as part of a larger meal alongside other mezze dips.

- SERVES 4

2 tomatoes, quartered
1 red onion, quartered
15 g (½ oz) parsley, stalks and leaves chopped
1 red chilli
1 spicy green chilli (ideally a bird's-eye)
2 garlic cloves, roughly chopped
1 tablespoon pomegranate molasses
1 tablespoon tomato purée
1 teaspoon dried mint
2 tablespoons olive oil

- METHOD

Add everything to a food processor with a splash of water and blend for 1 minute, or until you have a smooth sauce.

Serve and get stuck in!

DIPPING SUGGESTION
Turkish bread.

1

Zesty Beetroot & Pistachio Dip

This vibrant and fresh dip is great for when you have plant-based friends round. If you want to spice it up, add a red chilli when blending.

- SERVES 2–3

1 tablespoon shelled pistachios
300 g (10 oz) cooked beetroot, roughly chopped
1 garlic clove
zest of 1 lemon, juice of ½
2 teaspoons dukkah
salt

- METHOD

Toast the pistachios in a dry frying pan over a medium-low heat for 3–4 minutes, then set aside to cool. Once cool, roughly chop.

Add the beetroot, garlic and half the lemon juice to a high-speed blender with a pinch of salt and blitz until smooth. Taste for seasoning, adding a little more lemon juice if needed to suit your taste buds.

Serve in a bowl garnished with the chopped pistachios and dukkah.

DIPPING SUGGESTION
Crunchy fresh crudités.

Miso Whipped Tofu with Chilli Candied Nuts

This dairy-free dip has moreish candied nuts to give it a sweet and spicy kick. The recipe makes more of these than you'll need so keep the rest for a tasty snack. You can always swap the miso paste for spicy Korean gochujang for even more heat.

- SERVES 2

2 tablespoons caster sugar
100 g (3½ oz) mixed nuts, roughly chopped
1–2 teaspoons crispy chilli oil, depending on how spicy you like it (I like to use Chiu Chow here)
300 g (10 oz) silken tofu, drained
2 teaspoons white miso
1 spring onion, finely sliced, to garnish

- METHOD

Heat a small nonstick frying pan over a medium-low heat. Once hot, add the caster sugar and 1 tablespoon water. Stir to dissolve, then add the chopped nuts and chilli oil. Cook for 3–4 minutes or until everything is well combined and the nuts have absorbed the sugar syrup. Remove from the heat and leave to cool.

Add the silken tofu and miso to a food processor and blend until really smooth, scraping the sides with a spatula as you go. Break up the chilli candied nuts.

Spoon the miso whipped tofu into your serving dish, then top with the chilli candied nuts and sliced spring onion.

DIPPING SUGGESTION
I love to eat this with prawn crackers or a veggie alternative.

Images overleaf →

1

2

Hummus Beiruti

This is a twist on the classic hummus, often found in Beirut. It's a spicier version made with green chillies and the added freshness of parsley. I love using this recipe when we have surprise guests coming over and no time to cook.

- SERVES 4–6

500 g (1 lb) ready-made hummus
2 garlic cloves, crushed or finely chopped
3–4 green chillies, finely chopped
handful of parsley sprigs, leaves chopped, stalks discarded (reserve some leaves to garnish)
4 tablespoons olive oil
juice of 1 lemon
salt and freshly ground black pepper

- METHOD

Tip the hummus in a bowl and give it a really good stir. Add the garlic and stir again.

Add the green chillies, parsley and olive oil to a mixing bowl and stir to combine.

Stir most of the chilli and parsley oil through the hummus, adding half the lemon juice and seasoning to taste. Taste and add more lemon juice if liked.

Spread the hummus into a serving dish, garnishing with the remaining chilli and parsley oil and parsley leaves.

DIPPING SUGGESTION
Pittas or flatbreads.

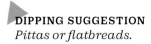

Black Olive Tapenade

This dip from Provence is a real classic, and you can make it as chunky or smooth as you like. If you prefer green olives, you can just swap them in – and leave out the anchovies if you don't like them.

- SERVES 3–4

100 g (3½ oz) black olives
50 g (2 oz) sun-dried tomatoes
20 g (¾ oz) capers, plus 1 teaspoon brine
1 garlic clove
2–3 anchovies (optional)
½ teaspoon dried oregano
2 tablespoons olive oil

- METHOD

Add the olives, sun-dried tomatoes, capers, garlic and anchovies (if using) to a food processor and blend until a chunky paste forms – you can either stop here or keep going for a smoother tapenade.

Transfer to a bowl, then stir in the oregano and olive oil. Add half the caper brine, then taste and add a little more if needed.

DIPPING SUGGESTION
Breadsticks.

Creamy Basil & Pecorino Dip

If you like a creamy pesto, this one's for you.

- SERVES 3–4

2 tablespoons pine nuts
50 g (2 oz) basil, leaves and stalks finely chopped (reserve some to garnish)
1 garlic clove, crushed or finely chopped
50 g (2 oz) Pecorino cheese, finely grated
3 tablespoons mayonnaise
100 g (3½ oz) soured cream
freshly ground black pepper

- METHOD

Toast the pine nuts in a dry frying pan over a medium-low heat for 3–4 minutes, then set aside to cool.

Add the basil to a bowl with the garlic and Pecorino and stir to combine.

Add the mayonnaise and soured cream and stir again, then transfer to a serving dish and serve garnished with the toasted pine nuts, a few chopped basil leaves and a good grind of black pepper.

DIPPING SUGGESTION
Italian-style breadsticks are perfect for scooping up this creamy dip.

Piri Piri Aioli

A very quick cheat's version of a piri piri aioli, this one is great to have on the table at a party, especially a barbecue.

• SERVES 4–6

250 ml (8 fl oz) vegetable oil
3 garlic cloves, finely chopped
1–2 red bird's-eye chillies
1 shallot, finely chopped
2 tablespoons red wine vinegar
1 tablespoon smoked paprika
1 teaspoon dried oregano
3 egg yolks
salt

• METHOD

Heat a drizzle of the oil in a small frying pan over a medium heat. Once hot, add the garlic, chillies and shallot, along with a pinch of salt, and cook for 4–5 minutes or until starting to soften. Add the red wine vinegar, smoked paprika and dried oregano and cook for another 2 minutes, then put to one side to cool. Once cool, transfer to a food processor, add a splash of water and blend until smooth – this is your piri piri paste. Transfer to a bowl and clean the food processor.

Add the egg yolks to the empty food processor with a pinch of salt. With the motor running, slowly pour in the remaining oil until the mixture has emulsified and has a mayonnaise-like thickness. Stir in the piri piri paste, transfer to a serving bowl and enjoy.

DIPPING SUGGESTION
Chicken wings, meat or veg skewers, fries or roast potatoes.

Dipping Oil

This recipe is a perfect example of 'Salt Fat Acid Heat', a term coined and popularized by Samin Nosrat. I've left it really loose so you can be creative and play around with what you have at home. Our fat here is going to be an oil, but your herbs, citrus and heat components can be changed to fit your mood, theme and cuisine! I've given you some suggestions, but go wild.

• SERVES 2–3

100 ml (3½ fl oz) extra virgin olive oil
handful of soft herbs of your choice (such as basil, parsley, mint and coriander), finely chopped
2–3 tablespoons citrus juice, vinegar or pomegranate molasses (you could even use pickle brine)
1–2 fresh chillies, finely chopped, or 1–2 teaspoons dried chilli flakes (or you can use black pepper or smoked paprika)
1–2 tablespoons finely chopped pickled and brined things (such as jalapeños, capers, pickled onions, sun-dried tomatoes and olives)
other mix-ins of your choice, such as a handful of chopped nuts or finely sliced spring onions, or 2–3 garlic cloves, finely chopped

• METHOD

Add your olive oil to a large shallow bowl, then top with your chosen mix-ins. I've suggested some possible combinations below; choosing a cuisine or global region to focus on helps!

SUGGESTED FLAVOUR COMBINATIONS

- *coriander, lime juice, jalapeños and garlic*
- *basil, garlic, balsamic vinegar and Parmesan*
- *dill, orange juice, shallots and capers*
- *mint, olives, sun-dried tomatoes and chopped almonds*

DIPPING SUGGESTION
Any type of bread to soak up all that lovely oil.

Avocado Green Goddess Dip

This vibrant, creamy dip is full of freshness from all the herbs and lots of zing from the lime juice.

- SERVES 3–4

2 avocados, peeled and pitted
50 g (2 oz) sliced jalapeños from a jar
juice of 2 limes
2 garlic cloves
20 g (¾ oz) fresh coriander, leaves and stalks roughly chopped
20 g (¾ oz) parsley, leaves roughly chopped and stalks discarded
20 g (¾ oz) basil, leaves and stalks roughly chopped
2 ice cubes
20 g (¾ oz) chives, finely chopped
1 tablespoon olive oil
salt and freshly ground black pepper

- METHOD

Add the avocados to a high-speed blender, along with the jalapeños, lime juice, garlic and all the herbs except the chives. Add the ice cubes and blend until smooth, then season to taste and scoop into a serving bowl.

In a separate bowl, mix the chives with the olive oil. Drizzle this herby oil over the dip to serve.

DIPPING SUGGESTION
Best enjoyed with steamed vegetables and/or crudités, but equally good with tortilla chips!

Classic Salsa Taquera

The classic red salsa you'll see on taco stands across Mexico (and much of the USA), but this one's on the milder side. By charring everything before blending, you get an added smokiness, but make sure to open a window or turn your kitchen extractor fan on high!

- SERVES 2–4

2 chiles de árbol
3 tomatoes, halved
1 onion, quartered
2 fresh jalapeños
3 garlic cloves, peeled and smashed
salt

- METHOD

Heat a heavy-based frying pan over a medium–high heat. Once hot, add all the ingredients except the salt and cook for 3–4 minutes to char all over, turning the vegetables regularly. Remove from the heat and set aside to cool.

Add everything to a high-speed blender and blend until smooth, adding a pinch of salt and a splash of water if needed. Transfer to a bowl to serve.

DIPPING SUGGESTION
Tortilla chips.

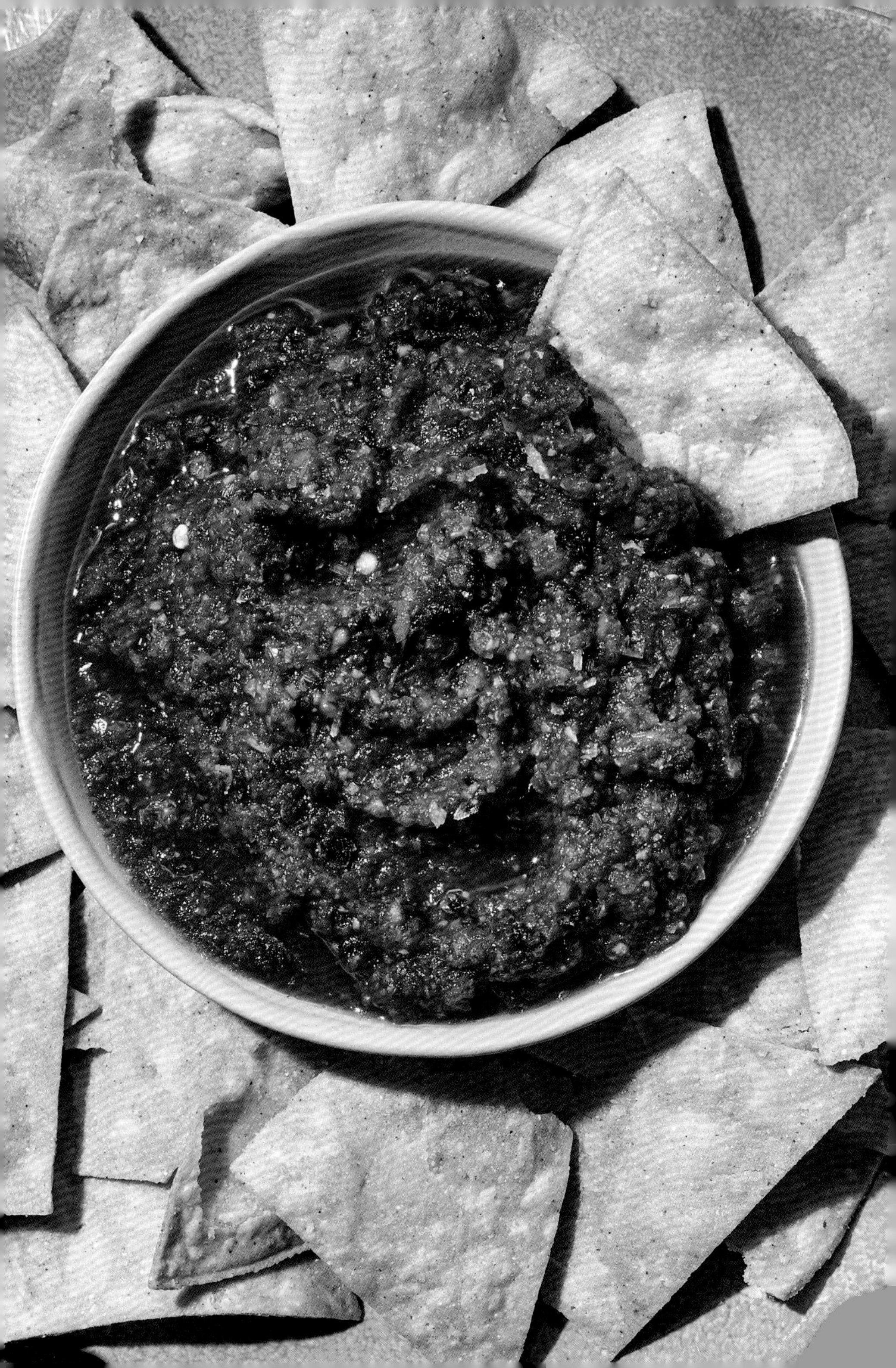

Graze

Whether you've got a picnic or barbecue to attend, or you've got friends coming over and want a grazing table, these dips are great for sharing. Make a few as part of your table, with a range of dippers.

Salsa Romesco

Traditionally served with calçots (a type of green onion), this classic Catalan dip is great with roasted veg.

- SERVES 4

40 g (1½ oz) dried breadcrumbs
100 g (3½ oz) almonds
100 g (3½ oz) blanched hazelnuts
750 g (1½ lb) roasted red peppers from a jar
4 teaspoons sherry vinegar
3 garlic cloves, chopped
2 teaspoons smoked paprika
160 g (5½ oz) sun-dried tomatoes, plus 1 tablespoon of their oil
160 ml (5½ fl oz) olive oil, plus extra to serve
salt and freshly ground black pepper

- METHOD

Add the breadcrumbs, almonds and blanched hazelnuts to a small nonstick frying pan over a medium heat and toast for 3–4 minutes or until browned all over. Set aside to cool.

Once cool, tip into a food processor. Add the roasted red peppers, sherry vinegar, garlic, paprika and sun-dried tomatoes, and blend until combined. Add the olive oil and sun-dried tomato oil, along with a generous pinch of salt and black pepper. Blend again until you have a chunky paste, then serve drizzled with a little more olive oil.

DIPPING SUGGESTION
A selection of grilled vegetables, such as big spring onions, courgettes, aubergines or Tenderstem broccoli.

Courgette Mutabal

This recipe is based on an aubergine mutabal, but with a courgette twist. Mutabal traditionally contains tahini, while baba ganoush does not. It also happens to be conveniently plant-based.

- SERVES 4

6 courgettes
2 garlic cloves, crushed or finely chopped
2 teaspoons sumac
2 tablespoons tahini
½ teaspoon dried mint
2 tablespoons extra virgin olive oil
1 teaspoon za'atar
salt

- METHOD

Line a baking sheet with tin foil. Arrange the courgettes on the baking sheet and place under a preheated hot grill for 20–30 minutes or until blackened all over, turning when required. Set aside to cool slightly.

Once the courgettes have cooled, halve them lengthways, then scoop out the flesh on to a chopping board. Roughly chop the flesh, then add to a mixing bowl (discarding any liquid) along with the garlic, sumac, tahini, mint, 1 tablespoon of the olive oil and a generous pinch of salt.

Serve the courgette mutabal topped with the remaining olive oil and the za'atar.

DIPPING SUGGESTION
Enjoy with flatbreads as part of a mezze table.

Confit Garlic & Oil Dip

This is a really simple method for making confit garlic, and it's a great way to use up extra garlic or any that's close to going off. You can swap the rosemary for thyme and add chopped chillies or black peppercorns for flavour variations.

- SERVES 2–3

2 garlic bulbs, cloves peeled
2 bay leaves
3 rosemary sprigs
100 ml (3½ fl oz) olive oil
salt

- METHOD

Add the garlic cloves to a small baking sheet with the bay leaves and rosemary, and sprinkle with a pinch of salt. Pour over the olive oil; everything should be submerged. Cover with tin foil and cook in a preheated oven, 160°C/140°C fan (325°F), Gas Mark 3, for 20–30 minutes, or until the garlic has softened.

Set aside to cool slightly before removing the herbs and mashing together the garlic, oil and salt with the back of a spoon. This is great to scoop up as it is, or you can use it as a spread or serve it drizzled over yogurt and other dips.

DIPPING SUGGESTION
Bread.

Gochujang (No-Cheese) Cheezy Dip

I love a cheese dip – you know the one you get in the cinema with nachos? I wanted to make a version that's accessible for anyone following a plant-based diet, but also just as delicious for those who aren't. I'm happy to say that this one hits the spot! I've added gochujang for smoky heat, but feel free to swap this for your favourite hot sauce.

- SERVES 4

200 g (7 oz) cashew nuts
2 tablespoons gochujang paste
2 tablespoons nutritional yeast
2 teaspoons dark soy sauce
1 teaspoon garlic powder
½–1 teaspoon smoked salt (optional)

- METHOD

Add the cashew nuts to a heatproof bowl and cover with 150 ml (¼ pint) boiling water. Set aside for 10–15 minutes to soak and soften.

Add the cashew nuts to a high-speed blender, along with half the soaking water. Blend until smooth, adding a splash more water if needed. Pour into a bowl.

Add the remaining ingredients and stir until combined. Serve while still warm with your dippers of choice!

DIPPING SUGGESTION
I love eating this with charred Padron peppers and, of course, tortilla chips.

Buffalo Chicken Dip

This one needs no introduction – buffalo chicken wings are famous worldwide and are one of my personal favourite treats. So a buffalo chicken dip is an obvious choice! If you want to swap out the meat here, chop some cauliflower into really small pieces, marinate it in extra hot sauce and roast at 200°C/180°C fan (400°F), Gas Mark 6, for 20 minutes, or until charred, then allow to cool and add it to the dip in place of the chicken.

- SERVES 3–4

100 g (3½ oz) cream cheese
50 g (2 oz) natural yogurt
50 ml (2 fl oz) hot sauce (I like Frank's)
400 g (13 oz) cooked chicken, finely chopped
2 celery sticks, finely chopped
handful of chives, finely chopped
50 g (2 oz) blue cheese, crumbled

- METHOD

Add the cream cheese, yogurt and hot sauce to a mixing bowl and stir until well combined.

Add the chopped cooked chicken and celery and half the chopped chives, then transfer to a serving bowl. Top with the crumbled blue cheese and remaining chives.

DIPPING SUGGESTION
Enjoy with a spoon, scooped into lettuce cups, or spread on crostinis or toast.

Caramelized Triple Onion & Soured Cream Dip

Triple onion power here, with caramelized onions, spring onions and onion powder for maximum flavour. Get your favourite crunchy crisps out and enjoy.

- SERVES 4

2 tablespoons vegetable oil
3 onions, finely sliced
3 spring onions, finely sliced
½ teaspoon salt
100 g (3½ oz) cream cheese
100 ml (3½ fl oz) Greek yogurt
1 teaspoon garlic powder
1 teaspoon onion granules
½ teaspoon white wine vinegar
1 tablespoon finely chopped pickled gherkins or cornichons
2 tablespoons finely chopped chives (optional)
freshly ground black pepper

- METHOD

Heat the oil in a nonstick frying pan over a medium-low heat. Once hot, add the onions and spring onions, along with 2 tablespoons water and the salt. Cook for 30–40 minutes, stirring regularly, until the onions have caramelized and turned a biscuit colour. Set aside to cool.

In a bowl, mix together the cream cheese, Greek yogurt, garlic powder and onion granules, then add the cooled caramelized onions (without their oil). Stir to combine, then add half the white wine vinegar and the chopped pickles. Taste for seasoning, adding more vinegar or salt if needed.

Serve topped with the chives, if liked, and a good grind of black pepper.

DIPPING SUGGESTION
Crostini or crunchy ridged potato crisps.

1

Tomatillo Salsa

Fresh tomatillos are quite hard to find in the UK and are usually quite expensive, so I've used canned ones here, which make a good alternative. If you want to make it spicier, increase your jalapeños! If you don't have a large pestle and mortar, then this can be made in a food processor.

- **SERVES 4**

50 g (2 oz) fresh coriander, both stalks and leaves finely chopped
1 fresh jalapeño, finely chopped
2 garlic cloves, finely chopped
½ onion, finely chopped
juice of 2 limes
760 g (1½ lb) can tomatillos, drained and roughly chopped
salt

- **METHOD**

Add the chopped coriander, jalapeño, garlic and onion to a large mortar, along with the lime juice and a pinch of salt. Use the pestle to pound to a smooth paste.

Add the chopped tomatillos and continue to pound until you have a chunky salsa – if you prefer a smoother salsa, just mash for longer. Taste for seasoning and enjoy!

DIPPING SUGGESTION
Serve with tortilla chips or as a part of a Mexican-inspired feast, alongside other dips!

S'ikil Pak

S'ikil pak is a classic pumpkin seed dip found in the Yucatán Peninsula, Mexico. Sometimes orange juice is added for sweetness. If you can't track down Scotch bonnets or find them too spicy, swap for an ordinary red chilli or even chilli flakes.

- **SERVES 4–6**

50 g (2 oz) pumpkin seeds
2 tomatoes
1 onion, peeled and quartered
5 garlic cloves (in their skins)
½ Scotch bonnet chilli (or 1 spicy red chilli)
juice of ½ lime
1 tablespoon vegetable oil
salt

- **METHOD**

Heat a large nonstick frying pan over a high heat. Once hot, add the pumpkin seeds and toast for 3–4 minutes or until charred all over, then transfer into a heatproof bowl and set aside.

Add the tomatoes, onion and garlic cloves to the pan and cook for 4–5 minutes, turning regularly, until they're well charred all over. Add to the same heatproof bowl, peeling the garlic cloves and discarding the skin, then leave to cool.

Once everything has cooled, tip into a food processor and add the chilli, lime juice, vegetable oil and a generous pinch of salt. Blend to form a smooth dip.

DIPPING SUGGESTION
Tortilla chips.

Images overleaf ⟶

1
2

3

3

Esquites

Esquites are one of my favourite Mexican street foods. In Mexico City, the stalls often have four or five bubbling pots with different flavours and toppings – with the rise of social media, some even have melted cheese and Taki crisps (spicy Mexican crisps) on top.

- **SERVES 4**

2 sweetcorn cobs
2 tablespoons salted butter
2 fresh jalapeños or green chillies, finely chopped
juice of 1–2 limes
4 tablespoons mayonnaise
50 g (2 oz) Parmesan cheese, grated
2 spring onions, sliced
Tajín (Mexican spice mix, optional)
salt

- **METHOD**

Stand a sweetcorn cob on its end, then use a sharp knife to carefully slice downwards to remove the kernels. Repeat with the other cob. Add the kernels to a saucepan with 300 ml (½ pint) water, season with a pinch of salt and bring to the boil. Cook for 15–20 minutes, or until the corn kernels have softened.

Once softened, stir in the butter, jalapeños and the juice of 1 lime. Remove from the heat, then add the mayonnaise and half the grated Parmesan. Taste for seasoning (adding more salt and/or lime if required), then transfer to a serving bowl and top with the remaining Parmesan, sliced spring onions and the Tajín (if using), or another squeeze of lime.

DIPPING SUGGESTION
This can be eaten with a spoon, or scooped up with crunchy tortilla chips.

← Image on previous page

Red & Green Mojo

Two recipes in one here, but both equally delicious. *Mojo rojo* and *mojo verde* are two amazing dips from the Canary Islands. I recommend serving them together with roasted baby potatoes, which is exactly how I ate them in Lanzarote.

- SERVES 4

For the red mojo
1 red pepper, halved and deseeded
1 garlic clove
1 tablespoon red wine vinegar
2 teaspoons smoked paprika
1 teaspoon ground cumin
1 red chilli
3 tablespoons olive oil, plus extra to serve
salt

For the green mojo
1 green pepper, halved and deseeded
50 g (2 oz) fresh coriander
1 garlic clove
1 tablespoon white wine vinegar
1–2 fresh jalapeños or green chillies
3 tablespoons olive oil, plus extra to serve

- METHOD

Line a baking sheet with nonstick baking paper. Add the halved red and green peppers to the baking sheet and bake in a preheated oven, 200°C/180°C fan (400°F), Gas Mark 6, for 20–30 minutes, or until roasted and charred. Remove from the oven and set aside to cool.

For the red mojo, add the charred red pepper and all the remaining ingredients to your food processor and blend until smooth, then transfer to a serving bowl.

For the green mojo, add the charred green pepper and all the remaining ingredients to your food processor and blend until smooth, then transfer to a serving bowl.

Garnish both with an extra drizzle of olive oil and enjoy!

DIPPING SUGGESTION
Roasted baby potatoes.

Preserved Lemon Tonnato

Tonnato is a classic Italian sauce typically served with veal in *vitello tonnato*, but I think it's actually really delicious as a stand-alone dip. The addition of preserved lemon is a little twist, as I love the depth of flavour it provides, but you can just use 1–2 tablespoons lemon juice instead if you prefer.

- SERVES 4

2 × 115 g (4 oz) cans tuna in oil (I like Ortiz)
2 preserved lemons (about 40 g/1½ oz each), finely chopped and seeds discarded, plus 1 teaspoon of their brine
2 garlic cloves, peeled
2 teaspoons capers
2 small shallots, peeled and roughly chopped
4 tablespoons mayonnaise
2 tablespoons olive oil
salt and freshly ground black pepper

- METHOD

Tip the tuna and its oil into a food processor. Add the remaining ingredients and blend until smooth. Taste and add salt if needed. Season with black pepper and serve.

DIPPING SUGGESTION
Herby crostini or a selection of crunchy crudités.

Salmorejo Dip

Salmorejo comes from Andalucía in Spain and is traditionally served as a cold soup. I've made it a bit thicker here so it's easily scoopable. To keep this vegetarian, leave out the Serrano ham or swap for green olives if liked.

- SERVES 2–4

250 g (8 oz) tomatoes
50 g (2 oz) stale bread
2 garlic cloves
50 ml (2 fl oz) extra virgin olive oil, plus extra for drizzling
1 tablespoon sherry vinegar
90 g (3¼ oz) Serrano ham, torn
1 egg
salt and freshly ground black pepper

- METHOD

Add the tomatoes, bread, garlic, olive oil and sherry vinegar to a blender with a pinch of salt and pepper, and blend until smooth. You might need to add a splash of water to help it blend.

Heat a drizzle of olive oil in a small frying pan over a medium heat. Once hot, add the Serrano ham and cook for 2–3 minutes or until crisp all over, then set aside to cool.

Boil the egg in a saucepan of boiling water for 9 minutes until hard-boiled, then scoop out with a slotted spoon and transfer to a bowl of iced water to stop cooking. Once cool, peel and roughly slice the egg.

Scoop the contents of the blender into a serving bowl and top with a drizzle of olive oil, the sliced egg and the Serrano ham. Sprinkle over a little salt and black pepper to serve.

DIPPING SUGGESTION
Enjoy with a spoon or bread.

Htipiti

This classic Greek dip (sometimes known as *tirokafteri*) is made with feta and roasted red peppers, and it's such a winner on a mezze table. You can roast your own peppers if you prefer, but I find using ready-roasted peppers in jars such a great way to cheat!

- SERVES 2

100 g (3½ oz) feta, drained
2 garlic cloves, roughly chopped
1 teaspoon dried oregano
2 teaspoons smoked paprika
200 g (7 oz) roasted red peppers from a jar, roughly chopped
1 teaspoon red wine vinegar
salt and freshly ground black pepper

- METHOD

Crumble the feta into a food processor, then add the garlic, oregano and half the smoked paprika. Blend until smooth, then add the roasted red peppers and blend until just combined.

Transfer into your serving dish, then stir in the red wine vinegar and taste for seasoning. Add a final dusting of smoked paprika and enjoy.

DIPPING SUGGESTION
Bread.

Japanese-Style Potato Salad

There are hundreds of potato salad recipes from around the world, but this Japanese-style one has got to be one of my favourites. If you're vegetarian, you can leave out the ham – and it's quite typical to add sweetcorn in Japan, too, if you want a variation.

- SERVES 2–3

400 g (13 oz) potatoes, peeled and cut into small chunks
1 egg
½ cucumber (about 200 g/7 oz), finely diced
1 carrot, finely diced
2 spring onions, finely sliced
2 teaspoons rice vinegar
5 tablespoons Kewpie mayo (or 5 tablespoons regular mayonnaise mixed with 1 teaspoon white wine vinegar)
4 slices of honey roast ham, chopped (optional)
salt

To garnish
2 teaspoons black sesame seeds
½ teaspoon shichimi togarashi (Japanese seven-spice powder)

- METHOD

Add the potatoes to a large saucepan and cover with water. Season with salt and bring to the boil. Once boiling, reduce to a simmer, then cook for 8–10 minutes or until the potatoes are soft. Drain, then tip into a mixing bowl and mash until chunky. Set aside to cool.

Boil the egg in a saucepan of boiling water for 9 minutes until hard-boiled, then scoop out with a slotted spoon and transfer to a bowl of iced water to stop cooking. Once cool, peel and dice the egg.

Add everything except the garnishes to the potato bowl and mix. Taste for seasoning, then transfer to a serving dish, scatter over the sesame seeds and shichimi togarashi and serve.

DIPPING SUGGESTION
Enjoy with a spoon!

Cretan Paste (Girit Ezme)

We were served this dip as part of a breakfast spread recently in Istanbul, and its salty moreishness worked so well with the huge variety of sweet and savoury dishes given to us.

- SERVES 2–3

50 g (2 oz) shelled pistachios
1 garlic clove, crushed or finely chopped
15 g (½ oz) basil, leaves and stalks finely chopped
15 g (½ oz) parsley, leaves and stalks finely chopped, any thick stalks discarded
75 g (3 oz) feta cheese
50 g (2 oz) cottage cheese
1 tablespoon olive oil
freshly ground black pepper

- METHOD

Toast the pistachios in a dry frying pan over a medium heat for 3–4 minutes until toasted all over, then set aside to cool. Once cool, finely chop.

Add the garlic to a bowl with most of the chopped basil and parsley. Add the chopped pistachios, then crumble in the feta and cottage cheese and mix well until combined. Stir in the olive oil.

Season with black pepper and serve garnished with the reserved herbs.

DIPPING SUGGESTION
Bread or breadsticks, or enjoy as part of a large Turkish-inspired spread.

Feast

Make a few of these dips and serve them with a variety of different dippers to create a fabulous feasting spread for your guests.

Everything-but-the-Bagel Dip

Making bagels for a crowd is always messy, and they always end up stale or soggy – so why not just make a bagel dip instead? Feel free to scale up to make a larger platter, or swap the toppings for your favourite bagel flavours. Vegetarians can leave out the salmon or swap it for diced cooked beetroot or chopped hard-boiled eggs.

- SERVES 2

2 shallots, finely sliced
zest and juice of 2 limes
pinch of granulated sugar
325 g (11 oz) cream cheese
½ cucumber, quartered lengthways, then finely sliced
3 teaspoons baby capers
200 g (7 oz) smoked salmon, torn into small pieces
1–2 tablespoons pickled red chillies, finely sliced
salt

For the bagel seasoning
1 teaspoon black sesame seeds
1 teaspoon white sesame seeds
1 teaspoon onion granules
1 teaspoon garlic powder
1 teaspoon poppy seeds
½ teaspoon sea salt

- METHOD

Add the shallots to a sieve placed over a bowl and rinse with boiling water. Leave to drain, then tip the drained shallots into another bowl. Add the lime juice, sugar and a pinch of salt, stir to combine, then set aside for 15 minutes to pickle.

Meanwhile, combine the bagel seasoning ingredients in a small bowl.

When you're ready to serve, spread the cream cheese over your serving plate and scatter the pickled shallots, cucumber, capers and salmon over in a decorative way.

Garnish with the lime zest, pickled chillies and bagel seasoning, and serve.

DIPPING SUGGESTION
Bagel chips or crostini.

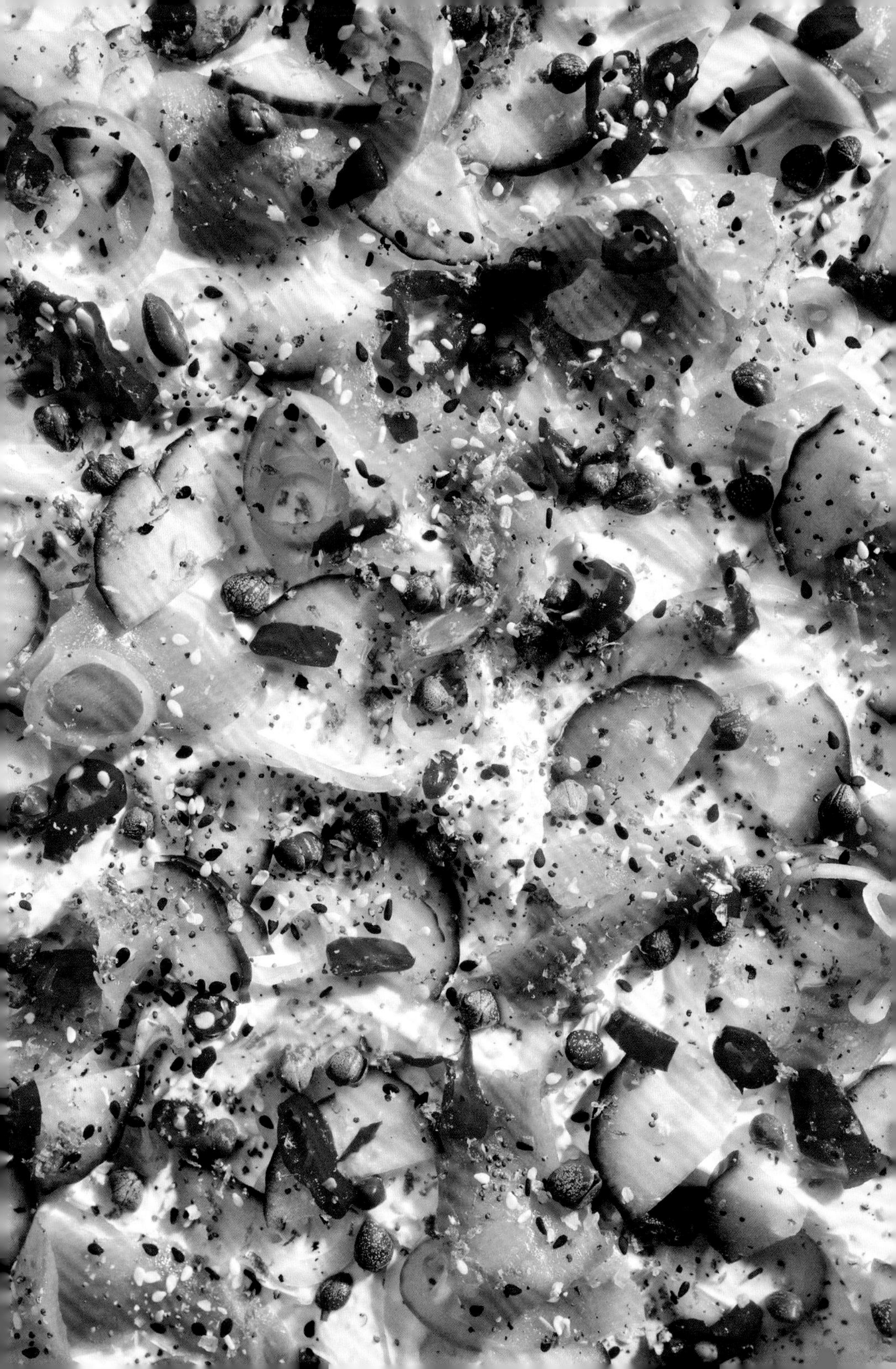

Zaalouk

This one-pot Moroccan aubergine and tomato dip can be eaten hot or cold. It's delicious mopped up with bread, and you can also add an egg on top for a more substantial meal.

- SERVES 4

2 tablespoons olive oil
4 tomatoes, chopped into 1 cm (½ inch) chunks
2 aubergines, peeled and chopped into 1 cm (½ inch) chunks
5 garlic cloves, finely chopped
2 teaspoons ground cumin
2 teaspoons paprika
1 teaspoon hot chilli powder (optional)
2 teaspoons white wine vinegar
25 g (1 oz) fresh coriander, leaves and stalks roughly chopped
salt

- METHOD

Heat the olive oil in a nonstick saucepan over a medium heat. Add the tomatoes, aubergines and garlic, followed by the spices and a generous pinch of salt. Cook for 10–15 minutes, stirring regularly or until the aubergines are soft and cooked through. Add a splash of water if needed.

Stir in the white wine vinegar and half the coriander and taste for seasoning. Serve garnished with the remaining coriander.

DIPPING SUGGESTION
Flatbreads.

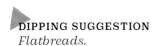

Turmeric & Macadamia Nut Dip

This dip was inspired by a dish I had in Malaysia called *ayam percik*, which is chicken grilled and roasted in a lemon grass, turmeric and coconut milk sauce. You can swap the macadamia nuts for blanched hazelnuts or unroasted peanuts. I love to eat this with grilled chicken or tofu skewers and a pickled cucumber salad.

- SERVES 2

1 tablespoon vegetable oil
1 banana shallot, sliced
1 lemon grass stick, finely chopped
2.5 cm (1 inch) piece of fresh root ginger, peeled and finely chopped
3 garlic cloves, finely chopped
1–2 green chillies, finely chopped
1 teaspoon ground turmeric
50 g (2 oz) macadamia nuts, roughly chopped
100 ml (3½ fl oz) coconut milk
1 tablespoon tamarind paste
2 tablespoons palm sugar (or soft light brown sugar)
salt

- METHOD

Heat the vegetable oil in a saucepan over a medium heat. Add the shallot, lemon grass, ginger, garlic and chillies, and cook for 6–8 minutes or until softened.

Add the turmeric and macadamia nuts, along with a pinch of salt, and cook for 1 minute before adding the coconut milk. Simmer for 5 minutes, then stir in the tamarind paste and palm sugar. Serve warm.

DIPPING SUGGESTION
Grilled chicken or tofu skewers.

Butter Chicken Dip

OK, I've taken the country's favourite Indian dish and turned it into a dip! I love serving this with some grilled Indian-spiced chicken, but if you're vegetarian, you can serve it with cubes of paneer, while plant-based people can swap to tofu. Kashmiri chilli powder is best for this, but if you can't find it use paprika instead.

- **SERVES 4**

2 tablespoons unsalted butter
1 tablespoon vegetable oil
2 teaspoons cumin seeds
2 onions, finely chopped
2.5 cm (1 inch) piece of fresh root ginger, peeled and finely chopped
6 garlic cloves, finely chopped
3–4 green chillies, finely chopped
1 teaspoon ground turmeric
2 teaspoons ground cumin
2 teaspoons ground coriander
4 teaspoons Kashmiri chilli powder
2 tablespoons tomato purée
2 teaspoons garam masala
3 tablespoons double cream

- **METHOD**

Heat a medium-sized saucepan over a medium heat. Once hot, add the butter, vegetable oil and cumin seeds. Once they start to sizzle, add the onions and cook for 5–6 minutes until softened.

Add the ginger, garlic and chillies, cook for another 2 minutes until softened, then add the turmeric, cumin, coriander and chilli powder, along with a splash of water, and stir. Cook for 2 minutes, then add the tomato purée and 100 ml (3½ fl oz) water and bring to a simmer. Cook for a further 5 minutes or until thickened, then stir in the garam masala and double cream. Enjoy warm.

DIPPING SUGGESTION
Grilled chicken, paneer or tofu.

Spicy Mayo Prawn & Cucumber Dip

I love eating this dip scooped onto little nori sheets, but it's equally good in lettuce or endive cups too. If you like really spicy food, you can also add your favourite chilli oil. Vegetarians can swap the prawns for cooked chopped mushrooms.

• SERVES 2

150 g (5 oz) cooked peeled prawns, finely chopped
3 tablespoons Kewpie mayonnaise (or 3 tablespoons regular mayonnaise mixed with ½ teaspoon white wine vinegar)
1–2 teaspoons sriracha
zest and juice of 1 lime
⅓ cucumber, finely chopped
handful of chives, finely chopped
salt

• METHOD

In a mixing bowl, combine the prawns with the mayonnaise, sriracha, lime juice and cucumber, stirring well. Taste for seasoning, adding salt if needed.

Transfer the spicy prawn dip to a serving bowl, top with the chopped chives and lime zest, then scoop up with your chosen dippers and enjoy!

DIPPING SUGGESTION
Nori sheets, or lettuce or endive cups.

Spinach & Mint Raita

A great way to jazz up that yogurt that's been sitting in your refrigerator – and to sneak some extra veg into your meals! Play around with the spices depending on what you've got at home, maybe bringing in fennel seeds or sesame seeds, you can swap the dried red chillis for chilli flakes, or just leave them out entirely if kids are eating with you.

- SERVES 4

300 g (10 oz) spinach
large handful of mint leaves, finely chopped
400 ml (13 fl oz) natural yogurt
1 teaspoon ground cumin
1 tablespoon vegetable or sunflower oil
2 teaspoons cumin seeds
2 teaspoons mustard seeds
2 dried red chillies, left whole
4 garlic cloves, finely sliced
salt

- METHOD

Heat a medium-sized frying pan over a medium heat. Once hot, add the spinach. Let it wilt, then remove from the heat and allow to cool.

Using a clean tea towel, squeeze any extra liquid from the spinach once it's cooled. Finely chop the spinach and add to a mixing bowl, along with the mint, natural yogurt and cumin. Season with salt and add a splash of water, then stir well to combine.

Wipe out the pan and return it to a medium heat, adding the oil. Once hot, add the cumin seeds, mustard seeds, dried red chillies and garlic, and sizzle for 2–3 minutes. Pour half this spiced oil mixture over the yogurt and stir.

Transfer the yogurt dip to a serving dish, and serve drizzled with the remaining spiced oil.

DIPPING SUGGESTION
Naan breads or poppadoms.

Ajo Blanco with Spicy Paprika Pulled Mushrooms

Ajo blanco is a Spanish soup that is served cold; it's not too dissimilar to *salmorejo* (see page 65), but it's made with almonds. It's the perfect basis for a creamy dip, and the spicy pulled mushrooms I've added here make a great topping.

- SERVES 3–4

100 g (3½ oz) blanched almonds
150 g (5 oz) stale bread
3 tablespoons milk (or plant-based milk)
1 tablespoon sherry vinegar
100 ml (3½ fl oz) extra virgin olive oil
salt and freshly ground black pepper

For the pulled mushrooms
150 g (5 oz) oyster mushrooms, shredded
3 tablespoons olive oil
2 teaspoons smoked paprika
1 teaspoon cayenne pepper

- METHOD

Toast the blanched almonds in a dry frying pan over a medium-low heat for 3–4 minutes, then set aside to cool.

Keep aside 15 g (½ oz) of the toasted almonds, then tip the rest into a high-speed blender, along with the stale bread, milk, sherry vinegar, olive oil and 50 ml (2 fl oz) water. Blend until smooth. Season, then transfer to a serving dish.

To make the mushrooms, heat a medium-sized frying pan over a high heat. Once hot, add the shredded mushrooms. Cook for 4–5 minutes, turning regularly, or until any liquid they've released has evaporated. Add the olive oil, smoked paprika and cayenne pepper, along with a pinch of salt, and continue to cook until the mushrooms crisp up. Serve these on top of the ajo blanco, drizzling over any spicy oil remaining in the pan. Chop the reserved toasted almonds and scatter them over the top.

DIPPING SUGGESTION
Enjoy with a spoon or with Spanish crackers.

1

Creamy Edamame & Wasabi Dip

Edamame are great as they are, but when blended, they become super creamy without the need to add any dairy. They're also very high in protein, so this dip is a great one to add to a plant-based feasting table. The almonds can be swapped for hazelnuts or cashew nuts if you prefer.

- **SERVES 2–4**

200 g (7 oz) frozen podded edamame beans, defrosted
40 g (1½ oz) blanched almonds
2 spring onions, finely sliced, whites and greens kept separate
1 small garlic clove, crushed or finely chopped
1–2 teaspoons wasabi paste
2 tablespoons Japanese pickled ginger
1 teaspoon sesame oil
salt

- **METHOD**

Place the edamame and blanched almonds in separate saucepans filled with salted water and bring both to the boil. Once boiling, reduce to a simmer, then cook for 2–3 minutes. Drain into two separate colanders and rinse until cool.

Add the drained almonds to a high-speed blender, along with the spring onion whites, garlic and 100 ml (3½ fl oz) water. Blend until smooth. Next add most of the edamame (reserving a handful to garnish) and pulse for 2–3 seconds – we want them to stay chunky. Add more water if needed. Taste for seasoning and stir in 1 teaspoon of the wasabi, then taste and add more if needed.

Serve the dip topped with the reserved edamame, spring onion greens and the Japanese pickled ginger, with the sesame oil drizzled over the top.

DIPPING SUGGESTION
Asian crackers, potato crisps or breadsticks.

Garlic Butter Beans with XO Chinese Sausage

Chinese sausage (called *lap cheong*) is easily available in Asian supermarkets, where you'll find it in the refrigerator section. It's slightly sweeter than its Western counterparts, but is so full of flavour. I use XO sauce a lot to add a smokiness to my dishes, and I think it works really well here. I like to serve this dip warm – and it's very good loaded on to prawn crackers!

• SERVES 2

1 tablespoon sesame oil
2 spring onions, finely chopped, greens and whites kept separate
3 garlic cloves, finely chopped
1 cm (½ inch) piece of fresh root ginger, peeled and finely chopped
400 g (13 oz) can butter beans, drained
2 Chinese sausages (*lap cheong*), sliced
2 tablespoons XO sauce
salt

• METHOD

Heat the sesame oil in a small frying pan over a medium heat. Once hot, add the spring onion whites, garlic and ginger, and cook for 3–4 minutes or until softened.

Add the butter beans, along with a pinch of salt and a splash of water, and cook for another 5 minutes, or until the beans have softened. Transfer to a bowl and set aside.

Wipe out the pan, then return it to a medium heat. Add the sliced sausages and cook for 5–6 minutes or until crispy. Stir in the XO sauce and continue to cook for another 1–2 minutes.

Meanwhile, mash the beans until chunky and transfer to a serving bowl. Serve topped with the crispy XO sausage and spring onion greens.

DIPPING SUGGESTION
Enjoy with a spoon, scooped into prawn crackers or with breadsticks.

Images overleaf →

1

2

Coconut & Spiced Black Bean Dip with Pineapple Salsa

The fresh pineapple salsa works really well here with the creamy beans, but canned pineapple would work too. Not a fan of pineapple? Swap to mango or even kiwi for a zesty kick! Try and find authentic Jamaican jerk seasoning if you can, as supermarket options can lack flavour.

- SERVES 2

1 tablespoon vegetable oil
2 spring onions, finely sliced, whites and greens kept separate
1 garlic clove
400 g (13 oz) can black beans, drained
1 tablespoon Jamaican jerk seasoning
150 ml (¼ pint) coconut milk
salt

For the pineapple salsa
100 g (3½ oz) pineapple flesh, finely diced
1–2 red chillies (depending on how spicy you like it), finely chopped
zest and juice of ½ lime
1 teaspoon olive oil

- METHOD

Heat the oil in a medium-sized saucepan over a medium heat. Once hot, add the spring onion whites and garlic, and cook for 2–3 minutes or until starting to soften.

Add the black beans and jerk seasoning, along with a pinch of salt. Pour in 100 ml (3½ fl oz) of the coconut milk and a splash of water, and cook for 10–12 minutes or until the beans have softened. Mash roughly and stir in the remaining coconut milk, then set aside.

Meanwhile, combine your pineapple salsa ingredients in a bowl with the spring onion greens and season with a pinch of salt.

Serve the mashed black beans with the pineapple salsa on top.

DIPPING SUGGESTION
Plantain chips or with a spoon!

Thai Red Curried Sweet Potato Dip

This dip was inspired by Thai red curry, but I wanted to make it more filling, so I added the sweet potato. To make this dip vegan, use plant-based milk and vegan Thai red curry paste.

- SERVES 2–3

400 g (13 oz) sweet potato, peeled and chopped into small pieces
1 tablespoon Thai red curry paste
2 tablespoons crunchy peanut butter
2 tablespoons milk
1 tablespoon vegetable oil
handful of Thai basil leaves
1 red chilli, finely sliced
salt

- METHOD

Line a baking sheet with nonstick baking paper.

Arrange the chopped sweet potato on the baking sheet and roast in a preheated oven, 200°C/180°C fan (400°F), Gas Mark 6, for 15 minutes, then add the red curry paste and mix well. Roast for another 10 minutes, then allow to cool.

Once cooled, add the sweet potato chunks to a high-speed blender, along with the peanut butter, milk and 100 ml (3½ fl oz) water. Blend until smooth, adding more water if needed, then taste for seasoning, adding salt if necessary. Transfer to a serving bowl.

Heat the oil in a small frying pan over a medium-low heat. Once hot, add the Thai basil leaves and sliced chilli, and fry for 2–3 minutes until crisp. Spoon over the dip to serve.

DIPPING SUGGESTION
Asian crackers or crispbreads.

Carrot & Radish Tarator

A *tarator* is a type of Turkish dip that usually contains walnuts and yogurt. It comes in many forms; one popular type contains carrot. I've added sliced radishes here for a peppery kick and walnuts for a good crunch.

- SERVES 3–4

100 g (3½ oz) walnuts
3 tablespoons olive oil
1 onion, sliced
200 g (7 oz) carrots, julienned or grated
100 g (3½ oz) radishes, julienned
3 garlic cloves, finely chopped
150 ml (5 fl oz) natural yogurt (or plant-based alternative)
handful of parsley, leaves finely chopped, stalks discarded
salt and freshly ground black pepper

- METHOD

Toast the walnuts in a dry frying pan over a medium-low heat for 3–4 minutes, then set aside to cool. Once cool, roughly chop.

Heat 2 tablespoons of the oil in the frying pan over a medium heat. Once hot, add the onion, along with a pinch of salt, and fry for 8–10 minutes or until golden and softened. Transfer to a bowl and set aside.

Return the pan to a medium heat and add the remaining olive oil. Add the carrots and radishes and cook for 3–4 minutes, then add the garlic and cook for a further 30 seconds. Remove from the heat and set aside to cool.

In a bowl, combine the natural yogurt with half the chopped walnuts and the cooled carrot and radish mixture. Season with salt and pepper.

Serve the dip topped with the cooked onions, chopped parsley and remaining walnuts.

DIPPING SUGGESTION
Enjoy as part of a larger Turkish-inspired spread with Turkish breads and grilled vegetables and meats.

Miso Mushroom & Whisky Pâté

Roasting the mushrooms and adding the miso and whisky gives some serious umami to this vegetarian pâté.

- SERVES 2

50 g (2 oz) dried shiitake mushrooms
500 g (1 lb) mixed fresh mushrooms, torn
2 banana shallots, sliced
2 garlic cloves, roughly chopped
2 tablespoon olive oil, plus extra to serve
2 tablespoons whisky
1 tablespoon miso paste
200 g (7 oz) cream cheese
handful of chives, chopped
freshly ground black pepper

- METHOD

Put the dried shiitake mushrooms into a bowl and pour over enough boiling water to cover. Leave to soak for 20 minutes.

Meanwhile, line a baking sheet with nonstick baking paper and scatter over the mixed mushrooms. Roast in a preheated oven, 200°C/180°C fan (400°F), Gas Mark 6, for 5 minutes, then add the shallots and garlic, along with the olive oil and a large pinch of black pepper. Cook for a further 5 minutes, then remove the baking sheet from the oven, drizzle over the whisky and set aside to cool completely.

Tip the cooled contents of the baking sheet, including any liquid, into a food processor and blend until combined.

Drain the shiitake mushrooms, reserving half a mug of the soaking liquid. Add the drained shiitake mushrooms to the food processor, along with the miso paste, cream cheese and a splash of the soaking liquid, and blend again until you have a chunky paste. Add more liquid if needed.

Taste for seasoning, then serve garnished with a drizzle of olive oil, the chopped chives and a final grind of black pepper.

DIPPING SUGGESTION
I love eating this with super-crusty bread or as part of a veggie grazing board.

Cottage Cheese & Salsa Macha

Salsa macha originates in Veracruz, Mexico. While it's technically a salsa, it's a bit different as it's oil based. You can enjoy it on its own, but it's particularly delicious drizzled over something creamy like cottage cheese. Use 2 dried chipotle chillies if guajillo chillies aren't available. Store any leftovers in a sterilized jar in the refrigerator for up to 4 weeks.

- **SERVES 4**

200 ml (7 fl oz) sunflower or vegetable oil
4 garlic cloves, peeled and smashed
2 tablespoons sesame seeds
2 tablespoons pumpkin seeds
2 tablespoons sunflower seeds
100 g (3½ oz) peanuts
2 ancho chillies, deseeded and finely chopped
4 guajillo chillies, deseeded and finely chopped
1 tablespoon cider vinegar
1 teaspoon salt
300 g (10 oz) cottage cheese

- **METHOD**

Pour the oil into a medium-sized saucepan. Add the garlic and place over a medium-low heat. Just before it starts to spit, reduce the heat to a simmer, then cook for 2–3 minutes or until fragrant.

Stir in the sesame seeds, pumpkin seeds, sunflower seeds, peanuts and chopped chillies, and continue to simmer for a further 5 minutes or until the seeds and nuts start to brown. Remove from the heat, stir in the cider vinegar and salt, then leave to cool.

Once cool, scoop out the solids using a slotted spoon and add them to a food processor. Blend until you have a chunky paste, then return this to the oil and stir to combine. Taste for seasoning.

When you're ready to serve, add the cottage cheese to your serving dish, then drizzle over 3–4 tablespoons of the salsa macha – or as much as you like!

DIPPING SUGGESTION
Crispbreads or crudités.

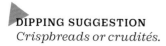

Skordalia

This garlicky Greek dip is sometimes made with bread and walnuts, but this version is made with potatoes. The blending creates a creamy, emulsified dip that is really addictive.

- SERVES 2

300 g (10 oz) potatoes, peeled and chopped into small pieces
4 garlic cloves, 2 left whole and 2 finely sliced
1 tablespoon red wine vinegar
4 tablespoon extra virgin olive oil, plus extra to serve
handful of parsley leaves, finely chopped
salt

- METHOD

Bring a saucepan of salted water to the boil. Add the potatoes and cook for 6–8 minutes or until very soft, then drain and mash. Set aside.

Meanwhile, add the 2 whole garlic cloves to a high-speed blender, along with the red wine vinegar and 3 tablespoons extra virgin olive oil. Blend until you have a paste. Add the mashed potatoes and a pinch of salt and blend again, adding a splash of water if needed.

Heat the remaining olive oil in a frying pan over a medium heat. Once hot, add the sliced garlic and cook for 3–4 minutes, or until starting to crisp up.

Serve the skordalia garnished with the crispy garlic, a drizzle of olive oil and the chopped parsley.

DIPPING SUGGESTION
Enjoy with a spoon or pitta chips.

Crunchy Chicken Caesar Dip

I like to go fully loaded with this dip, but you can tailor it to suit your tastes. Don't like anchovies? Leave them out. Fancy extra bacon? Go for it!

- SERVES 4–6

8 tablespoons mayonnaise
4 anchovies, chopped
2 garlic cloves, crushed or finely chopped
2 tablespoons lemon juice
200 g (7 oz) shredded cooked chicken
2 celery sticks, finely chopped
2 tablespoons capers, roughly chopped
4 tablespoons ready-made crispy fried onions
50 g (2 oz) cooked crispy bacon rashers, roughly chopped
handful of chives, chopped
salt and freshly ground black pepper

For the croutons
1 slice of sourdough bread, torn into small bite-sized chunks
2 tablespoons olive oil

- METHOD

First make the croutons. Line a baking sheet with nonstick baking paper. Add the torn bread and drizzle over the olive oil, tossing to coat. Bake in a preheated oven, 200°C/180°C fan (400°F), Gas Mark 6, for 8–10 minutes, or until crispy, stirring the croutons halfway through. Set aside to cool.

Combine the mayonnaise, anchovies and garlic in a bowl, then stir in half the lemon juice. Once combined, add the chicken, celery and capers. Stir and taste for seasoning, adding a good grind of black pepper and more lemon juice if needed.

Just before serving, stir through the croutons and top the dip with the crispy fried onions, crispy bacon and chives.

DIPPING SUGGESTION
Little gem lettuce cups.

Impress

These are the dips to turn to when you need to elevate a meal with something a bit more indulgent on the table. They work well as dinner-party starters or as sharers, but make sure you go for premium dippers.

Whipped Feta & Burned Tomatoes with Ginger & Spring Onion Dressing

A bit of a cross-cuisine dish. The whipped feta is salty and creamy, and it's topped with a ginger and spring onion oil often served with dishes like Hainanese chicken.

- SERVES 2

100 g (3½ oz) cherry tomatoes
100 g (3½ oz) feta
100 ml (3½ fl oz) Greek yogurt
1 teaspoon balsamic vinegar

For the ginger & spring onion dressing
2.5 cm (1 inch) piece of fresh root ginger, peeled and finely chopped
2 garlic cloves, finely sliced
2 spring onions, finely sliced, whites and greens kept separate
75 ml (3 fl oz) vegetable oil
salt

- METHOD

To make the dressing, add the ginger, garlic and spring onion whites to a heatproof bowl and season with a pinch of salt. Pour the vegetable oil into a small saucepan and heat over a medium-high heat until just smoking, then carefully pour this over the aromatics in the bowl (they should sizzle). Set aside to cool.

Heat a small nonstick frying pan over a medium-high heat and add the cherry tomatoes. Once they start to char all over, add 2–3 tablespoons water and continue to cook for another 3–4 minutes or until they are almost bursting. Remove from the heat and set aside.

Add the feta and Greek yogurt to a food processor and blend for 1–2 minutes or until really smooth.

To serve, spoon the whipped feta into a bowl. Top with the burned tomatoes and drizzle over 2–3 teaspoons of the dressing (any leftovers will keep in the refrigerator for up to 5 days). Finish with the balsamic vinegar and sliced onion greens.

DIPPING SUGGESTION
Seeded crackers.

Sichuan Burned Aubergines

This dip is inspired by one of my favourite Sichuan dishes, known as 'fish fragrant aubergine'. The smoky spiciness is offset by the unique flavour of the black vinegar. It can be eaten warm or cold.

- SERVES 2

2 aubergines
2 teaspoons sesame oil
2.5 cm (1 inch) piece of fresh root ginger, peeled and finely chopped
2 garlic cloves, finely chopped
2 spring onions, finely sliced, greens and whites kept separate
2 tablespoons Chinese chilli bean sauce
1 teaspoon dark soy sauce
½–1 teaspoon Chinese black vinegar (or malt vinegar)

- METHOD

Line a baking sheet with tin foil.

Arrange the aubergines on the prepared baking sheet and place under a preheated hot grill for 10–15 minutes, or until blackened all over, turning them regularly. Set them aside to cool slightly, then carefully halve each aubergine lengthways. Scoop out the flesh and finely chop.

Heat a nonstick frying pan over a medium heat. Once hot, add 1 teaspoon of the sesame oil, along with the ginger, garlic and spring onion whites. Stir-fry for 3–4 minutes, or until starting to soften, then add the chilli bean sauce and soy sauce. Stir to combine, then add in the chopped aubergine.

Serve either warm or cold, drizzled with the remaining sesame oil and the Chinese black vinegar (to taste), and with the spring onion greens scattered over the top.

DIPPING SUGGESTION
Prawn crackers, lettuce cups or cucumbers.

Easy Béarnaise Dip

I love getting Béarnaise sauce with my steak, but always prefer it when it's a bit thicker so I can dip the steak in – so that's where this recipe came from. If you're vegetarian, it's equally delicious with roasted mushrooms or simply crispy fries!

- **SERVES 2**

1 shallot, finely sliced
100 ml (3½ fl oz) white wine vinegar
1 tablespoon black peppercorns
1 teaspoon cumin seeds
4 tarragon sprigs
2 egg yolks
150 g (5 oz) ghee (clarified butter), melted
salt and freshly ground black pepper

- **METHOD**

Add the shallot, white wine vinegar, black peppercorns, cumin seeds and 2 of the tarragon sprigs to a small saucepan and bring to the boil. Cook for 4–5 minutes or until reduced by half, then strain into a heatproof jug – this is your reduction.

Add the egg yolks to a bowl that fits snugly over a saucepan of simmering water (without actually touching the water) and whisk the yolks to combine. Slowly pour in the reduction, whisking all the while.

Next, slowly pour in the melted ghee, and keep whisking until the mixture thickens to the consistency of double cream (this might take 5–10 minutes).

Carefully remove from the heat and season with salt. Chop the leaves of the remaining tarragon sprigs and stir these through. Serve your dip topped with a good grind of black pepper – and enjoy!

DIPPING SUGGESTION
Steak and fries.

Bloody Maria Prawn Cocktail Dip

This was inspired by the classic prawn cocktail, but also my favourite brunch cocktail – the Bloody Maria (a Bloody Mary with tequila instead of vodka). Best eaten with cooked seafood like big, juicy king prawns or langoustines, and presented in your most retro glasses. Serve with avocado and lettuce, too, if liked!

- SERVES 2

100 g (3½ oz) mayonnaise
2 tablespoons tomato ketchup
½–1 teaspoon Mexican hot sauce
2 tablespoons tequila
1 teaspoon Worcestershire sauce
juice of ½ lime

- METHOD

Combine all the ingredients in a bowl and stir to combine. Taste and add a little more lime juice if needed, then serve.

DIPPING SUGGESTION
Big king prawns, langoustines, crab or lobster.

Beet/Beef Tartare

I've left this one a little bit open so you can tailor it to suit yourself and your guests. The recipe works with both beef and beetroot.

- SERVES 2

200 g (7 oz) cooked beetroot, finely diced, or 200 g (7 oz) high-quality, very fresh fillet steak, finely diced
2 shallots, 1 finely chopped and 1 sliced into rings (to garnish)
1 teaspoon Dijon mustard
2 teaspoons horseradish
2 tablespoons capers, finely chopped
3 tablespoons cornichons, finely chopped
handful of chives, finely chopped
25 g (1 oz) Parmesan cheese, grated
2 egg yolks
salt and freshly ground black pepper

- METHOD

In a bowl, combine the beetroot or beef with the chopped shallot, mustard, horseradish, capers, cornichons and half the chopped chives. Mix well and season with a pinch of salt and pepper.

For a classic serve, place a cookie cutter on each of your serving plates and spoon the tartare mixture in, pressing down with a spoon. Remove the cookie cutters, then use your spoon to make a small indentation in the centre of each portion. Sprinkle over the sliced shallots, remaining chives and Parmesan, then place the egg yolks in the indents. Finish with a good grind of black pepper and enjoy!

DIPPING SUGGESTION
Something crunchy, like rye toast or crackers.

Date & Sumac Baked Camembert

Baked camembert isn't just for Christmas! You can eat it all year round, and changing the toppings keeps it interesting. Date syrup is pretty easy to get hold of nowadays, but if you can't find it, a thick maple syrup or golden syrup would be a good substitute. The sumac balances out the sweetness and the chilli kick.

- SERVES 2

250 g (8 oz) camembert
3 tablespoons date syrup
50 g (2 oz) mixed nuts, finely chopped
½ teaspoon chilli flakes
1 teaspoon sumac
1 tablespoon olive oil

- METHOD

Remove the plastic packaging from your camembert, then pop the cheese back in its box and place it on a baking sheet.

Cut a cross-hatch pattern into the top of the cheese with a sharp knife, then bake in a preheated oven, 180°C/160°C fan (350°F), Gas Mark 4, for 10 minutes.

Meanwhile, in a small bowl, mix 2 tablespoons of the date syrup with the chopped nuts, chilli flakes and sumac. Spoon this mixture over the camembert, then drizzle over the olive oil and remaining date syrup. Return the cheese to the oven for a further 5 minutes or until bubbling. Leave to cool for a few minutes before tucking in.

DIPPING SUGGESTION
Breadsticks or thick crackers.

Mushroom Fatteh

You can find variations of *fatteh* across the Levant and Egypt. Households will make their own version depending on their cuisine, but they usually follow a similar format of layering crisp bread, meat or vegetables and a tahini-based yogurt. My version uses mushrooms, which I think work really well here – I like to use a mix of oyster, chestnut and shiitake, but you can use whichever you like.

- SERVES 2

2 Middle Eastern-style flatbreads
2 tablespoons vegetable oil
500 g (1 lb) mixed mushrooms, torn into small pieces
2 tablespoons tomato purée
2 teaspoons ground cumin
300 ml (½ pint) natural yogurt
2 tablespoons tahini
2 tablespoons lemon juice
2 garlic cloves, finely chopped
4 tablespoons salted butter
4 tablespoons pine nuts
2 teaspoons sumac
salt

• **METHOD**

Line a baking sheet with nonstick baking paper. Tear the flatbreads into small bite-sized pieces and add them to the baking sheet. Drizzle over 1 tablespoon of the vegetable oil and toss to coat, then bake in an oven preheated to 200°C/180°C fan (400°F), Gas Mark 6, for 10–12 minutes until crispy, stirring halfway through.

Meanwhile, heat the remaining vegetable oil in a medium-sized frying pan over a medium-high heat. Once hot, add the mushrooms, along with a pinch of salt, and cook for 5–6 minutes. Stir in the tomato purée, ground cumin and 50 ml (2 fl oz) water. Cook for another 2 minutes, then turn off the heat.

In a bowl, mix together the yogurt, tahini, lemon juice and garlic. Season with a pinch of salt.

Arrange half the crispy flatbread pieces across the bottom of your serving dish, then top with the mushrooms. Drizzle over the tahini yogurt and top with the remaining flatbread pieces.

Wipe your mushroom pan clean, then place it over a medium-low heat. Add the butter. Once it's melted, add the pine nuts and increase the heat to medium, so that the butter starts to brown and the pine nuts sizzle. After about 2 minutes, once the butter is a dark biscuit colour, remove from the heat and drizzle the butter and pine nuts over the top of the dish. Sprinkle with the sumac and enjoy.

DIPPING SUGGESTION
With a spoon!

Lobster Roll Dip

Inspired by the classic lobster roll found along America's east coast, this dip is easy to make and can be prepared a day ahead of time. Swap the lobster for crab, or even prawns, if you prefer.

- SERVES 2

2 fresh or defrosted lobster tails
1 tablespoon olive oil
2 shallots, finely chopped
2 teaspoons Old Bay Seasoning
½–1 teaspoon cayenne pepper
½ teaspoon mustard powder
1 teaspoon Worcestershire sauce
1 celery stick, finely chopped
100 g (3½ oz) mayonnaise
zest of 1 lemon, juice of ½
handful of parsley, leaves finely chopped, stalks discarded
2 tablespoons unsalted butter
3 tablespoons dried breadcrumbs
2 tablespoons grated Parmesan cheese
salt and freshly ground black pepper

- METHOD

Using a sharp pair of kitchen scissors, carefully cut each lobster tail in half lengthways, scoop out the meat and chop it into large bite-sized pieces.

Heat the oil in a nonstick frying pan over a medium heat. Once hot, add the chopped shallots and a pinch of salt. Cook for 4–5 minutes or until softened, then add the Old Bay Seasoning, cayenne pepper, mustard powder and Worcestershire sauce. Stir to combine, then add the lobster chunks. Continue to cook for a further 3–4 minutes or until the meat is just cooked, then remove from the heat and leave to cool.

Once cool, stir in the celery, mayonnaise, lemon zest and juice and half the parsley. Spoon into your serving dish and wipe the frying pan clean.

Return the frying pan to a medium heat. Once hot, add the butter and let it melt. Stir in the breadcrumbs, a pinch of salt, the Parmesan and the remaining parsley. Cook for 3–4 minutes or until golden brown. Spoon this over the lobster mixture, add a good grind of black pepper and enjoy!

DIPPING SUGGESTION
Toasted brioche.

Smashed Gilda on Ricotta

You'll find Gilda skewers (pepper, olive and anchovy skewers) on many wine bar menus these days – they originate in Spain. I wanted to take that salty pickled flavour and turn it into a dip.

• SERVES 4

1 tablespoon olive oil
50 g (2 oz) flaked almonds
500 g (1 lb) ricotta
100 g (3½ oz) pitted green olives, roughly chopped
50 g (2 oz) anchovies, 2–3 chopped and the rest left whole
100 g (3½ oz) guindilla chillies, roughly chopped
salt and freshly ground black pepper

• METHOD

Heat the olive oil in a small frying pan over a medium heat. Add the flaked almonds and cook for 2–3 minutes or until golden and toasted, stirring regularly. Set aside.

Spoon the ricotta into your serving dish and season. Add the olives, guindilla chillies and chopped anchovies, then garnish with the whole anchovies and serve topped with the flaked almonds.

DIPPING SUGGESTION
Toasted ciabatta or Italian crackers.

Seven-Layer Chaat Dip

Seven-layer dip, but make it chaat. Chaat is a type of Indian street food, where toppings vary but always incorporate the perfect balance of salty, sweet, sour, fresh and crunchy. In this recipe, I've taken the classic American seven-layer dip and transformed it into my version of *papdi chaat*. You can layer it in one big dish, or present it in individual dishes or glasses. *Papdis* are flat, crispy puris, and they are readily available from Indian supermarkets, as are nylon sev (a very thin form of sev) and chaat masala. Kashmiri chilli powder is best for this, but if you can't find it use paprika instead.

- **SERVES 4**

300 ml (½ pint) natural yogurt
pinch of granulated sugar
200 g (7 oz) *papdi chaat* puris
1 potato (about 300 g/10 oz), boiled and finely diced
400 g (13 oz) can chickpeas, drained
½ quantity Coriander Chutney (see page 22)
75 g (3 oz) tamarind chutney
1 tablespoon chaat masala
1 tablespoon Kashmiri chilli powder
1 green mango, peeled, pitted and finely chopped
100 g (3½ oz) pomegranate seeds
50 g (2 oz) nylon sev
handful of fresh coriander, leaves and stalks finely chopped
salt

For the spicy garlic sauce
50 g (2 oz) long red chillies
3 garlic cloves
1 teaspoon salt

1

2

3&4

- **METHOD**

In a high-speed blender, combine the ingredients for the spicy garlic sauce, and blend until smooth.

In a bowl, combine the yogurt and 3 tablespoons water with the sugar and a pinch of salt.

- **NOW START LAYERING UP THE DIP:**

1. Crush half the papdis and spread them out on the bottom of your serving dish.
2. Top with the diced potatoes and chickpeas, and season with salt.
3. Spoon over the coriander chutney, spicy garlic sauce and tamarind chutney.
4. Sprinkle over half the chaat masala and half the Kashmiri chilli powder.
5. Drizzle over the yogurt mixture.
6. Scatter over the green mango and pomegranate seeds.
7. Finish with the remaining chaat masala and Kashmiri chilli powder, followed by the remaining papdis (crushing as you sprinkle), nylon sev and coriander.

DIPPING SUGGESTION
With a spoon!

Image overleaf →

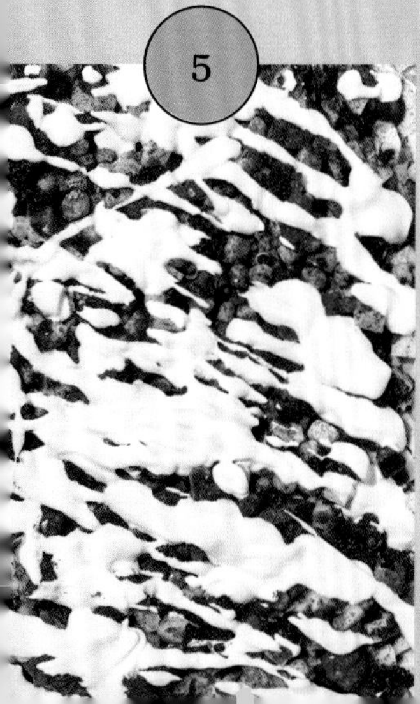

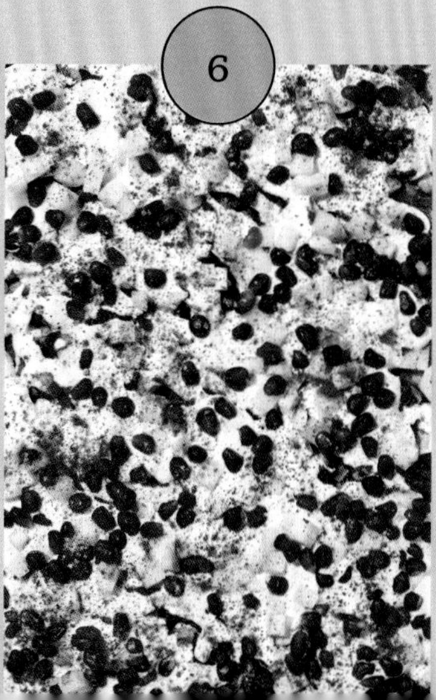

Crab & Kohlrabi Remoulade

This one's a riff on the classic French celeriac remoulade, using kohlrabi and crunchy green apple with the addition of crab. If you're not into crab, you can swap it for chopped prawns.

• SERVES 4

4 tablespoons mayonnaise
1 teaspoon Dijon mustard
4 tablespoons lemon juice
handful of dill, finely chopped
100 g (3½ oz) kohlrabi, peeled and finely chopped
1 green apple, cored and finely diced
100 g (3½ oz) cooked crab meat
salt and freshly ground black pepper

• METHOD

Add the mayonnaise, mustard and lemon juice to a mixing bowl and stir until well combined. Add half the dill, then stir in the kohlrabi, apple and crab. Taste for seasoning, adding a pinch of salt and black pepper.

Serve the dip topped with the remaining dill.

DIPPING SUGGESTION
Crusty French baguette slices, toasted and drizzled with oil.

Tuna & Kimchi Tartare

Tuna tartare might sound difficult, but as long as you can get hold of sushi-grade fish from your fishmonger, it's really easy. This one has a spicy twist.

- **SERVES 4**

2 tablespoons kimchi, finely chopped
1 teaspoon sesame oil
½–1 teaspoon light soy sauce
1 teaspoon sesame seeds, ideally a mix of black and white
200 g (7 oz) sushi-grade tuna, diced into fine cubes and kept in the refrigerator until needed
1 avocado, peeled, pitted and finely diced
1 tablespoon ready-made crispy fried onions

- **METHOD**

In a mixing bowl, combine the kimchi with the sesame oil, soy sauce and half the sesame seeds, then stir in the tuna.

Divide the tartare mixture between your plates (you can use a round cookie cutter if you want to shape the portions). Top with the remaining sesame seeds and crispy onions – and enjoy!

DIPPING SUGGESTION
Peppery shiso leaves, baby gem lettuce cups or endive cups.

Coconut Prawn Ceviche/Kinilaw

This recipe is inspired by the Filipino dish known as *kinilaw*. It's prepared in a similar way to ceviche, where the fish is cured in lime juice, but here the fish is traditionally cured in coconut vinegar. Use this if you can find it, otherwise a mild vinegar like rice vinegar or white balsamic will work.

- SERVES 2

165 g (5¾ oz) raw king prawns, peeled and roughly chopped
½ red onion, finely sliced
3 tablespoons coconut vinegar (see recipe introduction)
200 ml (7 fl oz) coconut milk
juice of 1 lime
1 hot red chilli, finely sliced
1 teaspoon soft light brown sugar
1 tablespoon fish sauce
1 teaspoon dark soy sauce
2.5 cm (1 inch) piece of ginger, peeled and finely chopped
½ cucumber, finely chopped
handful of fresh coriander, leaves and stalks finely chopped
salt

- METHOD

In a bowl, combine the prawns with the red onion, vinegar and a pinch of salt. Stir to combine, then set aside for 20 minutes to cure.

Meanwhile, in a second bowl, mix together everything else, except the coriander, with 50 ml (2 fl oz) water.

After 20 minutes, add the prawn mixture (including the vinegar) to this bowl and stir to combine. Season with salt to taste and stir through half the coriander, then serve topped with the remaining coriander.

DIPPING SUGGESTION
With a spoon, potato crisps or tortilla chips.

Burrata with Crispy Artichokes & Pistachio Gremolata

It really annoys me when restaurants don't season their burrata; while it's deliciously creamy in texture, it takes its flavour from its accompaniments. Here, roasted artichokes provide crunch and the dressing gives it a zesty kick.

- SERVES 4

280 g (9 oz) jar of artichokes, drained
40 g (1½ oz) shelled pistachios, roughly chopped
handful of parsley, leaves roughly chopped and stalks discarded
2 garlic cloves, crushed or finely chopped
zest and juice of 1 lemon
3 tablespoons olive oil
2 × 150 g (5 oz) burrata, drained
salt and freshly ground black pepper

- METHOD

Line a baking sheet with nonstick baking paper. Arrange the artichokes on the prepared sheet in a single layer and roast in a preheated oven, 200°C/180°C fan (400°F), Gas Mark 6, for 10–15 minutes or until crisp, adding the pistachios to the tray for the last 2 minutes.

In a bowl, combine the parsley, garlic, lemon zest and juice and the olive oil. Season with a pinch of salt and pepper and stir to combine. Add the toasted pistachios and set aside – this is your gremolata.

Add the burrata to your serving dish, then cut open. While they're still oozing out, top with the warm, crisp artichokes and drizzle over the pistachio gremolata to serve.

DIPPING SUGGESTION
Enjoy with olive or plain ciabatta crostinis.

Meals

These hearty dips are more filling and are best served as a delicious meal in themselves, alongside their suggested dippers.

Ful Medames

I love trying out local breakfasts on holiday. This was something I had in Cairo almost every day. You'll find tinned fava beans in your local international greengrocer, particularly if they stock Middle Eastern or Turkish foods. Shatta is a condiment found all over the Levant. This is best enjoyed with the suggested dippers, and we often make it for dinner because it's so easy but nutritious.

- SERVES 2

1 tablespoon vegetable oil
1 onion, finely chopped
1 green chilli, finely chopped
2 tomatoes, finely chopped
2 × 400 g (13 oz) cans fava beans, drained
2 teaspoons ground cumin
salt

For the green chilli shatta
1 garlic clove, roughly chopped
1–2 green chillies
2 tablespoons lemon juice
extra virgin olive oil

- METHOD

Heat the vegetable oil in a medium-sized saucepan over a medium heat. Once hot, add the onion and chilli, along with a pinch of salt, and cook for 4–5 minutes or until starting to soften.

Add the tomatoes with a splash of water, and cook for another 2–3 minutes or until the tomatoes start to break down. Add the drained fava beans, followed by the ground cumin, and cook for 3–4 minutes more. Add more water if needed, but the dish should be quite thick.

Meanwhile, combine the green chilli shatta ingredients in a mortar along with a pinch of salt, and pound with the pestle until it forms a chunky paste.

Serve the ful medames topped with the green chilli shatta.

DIPPING SUGGESTION
Boiled eggs, cucumbers, tomatoes, red onions and bread.

Poached Eggs with Tadka Butter

An Indian twist on the classic dish *çılbır*, or 'Turkish eggs'. Kashmiri chilli powder is mild but gives a beautiful red hue to your ghee; if you can't find it, use paprika instead. Fried eggs work well here too.

- SERVES 2

40 g (1½ oz) ghee (or unsalted butter)
10–12 curry leaves
1 teaspoon cumin seeds
½–1 teaspoon chilli flakes
1 teaspoon sesame seeds
½ teaspoon Kashmiri chilli powder
200 ml (7 fl oz) Greek yogurt
2 garlic cloves, crushed or very finely chopped
2 eggs
white wine vinegar
handful of fresh coriander, chopped (optional)
salt

- METHOD

Heat a small nonstick frying pan over a low–medium heat. Once hot, add the ghee and let it melt, then add the curry leaves, cumin seeds, chilli flakes, sesame seeds and Kashmiri chilli powder, along with a pinch of salt, and cook for 3–4 minutes or until fragrant.

In a bowl, stir together the Greek yogurt with the garlic and a pinch of salt, then divide between 2 shallow bowls.

Bring a saucepan of water to the boil. Once boiling, reduce to a simmer and add a dash of white wine vinegar and a pinch of salt. Gently stir the water to create a whirlpool, then crack in an egg. Cook for 3–4 minutes, then remove the egg with a slotted spoon. Repeat with the remaining egg. Drain the poached eggs well, then place them on top of the yogurt in the bowls. Drizzle with the spiced butter and scatter over the coriander, if liked.

DIPPING SUGGESTION
Sourdough toast.

Choriqueso

A Mexican street-food classic, this dip is not for the faint hearted. Eat soon after it's out of the oven to make the most of the cheesy goodness. You can swap the chorizo for mushrooms, which is often done in Mexico, and add sliced hot green chillies for more heat.

- SERVES 2

100 g (3½ oz) chorizo, finely chopped
1 onion, finely chopped
2–3 tablespoons sliced jalapeños from a jar, finely chopped
100 g (3½ oz) ready-grated mozzarella cheese
100 g (3½ oz) Cheddar cheese, grated

- METHOD

Heat a cast-iron pan (or an ovenproof frying pan) over a medium heat. Add the chorizo and cook for 4–5 minutes, or until it starts to crisp up and has released its oils. Remove the chorizo from the pan and set aside on a plate, leaving behind the oil.

Add the onion to the pan with the chorizo oil, still over a medium heat, and cook for 3–4 minutes or until softened. Stir through the chopped jalapeños, then remove the pan from the heat.

Return the chorizo to the pan and stir, then sprinkle over the mozzarella and Cheddar. Cook under a preheated hot grill for 3–4 minutes until the cheese is melted and bubbly. Set aside to cool slightly before dipping.

DIPPING SUGGESTION
Warm tortillas or tortillas chips.

Menemen

This is a classic Turkish breakfast item, but we often have it for dinner at our house. If you don't eat eggs, you could swap them for crumbled silken tofu.

- **SERVES 2**

1 tablespoon vegetable oil
1 onion, finely chopped
1 green pepper, cored, deseeded and finely chopped
200 g (7 oz) cherry tomatoes, quartered
1 tablespoon Turkish red pepper paste (use tomato purée if you can't find this)
1 teaspoon pul biber (use smoked paprika if you can't find this)
1 teaspoon paprika
½–1 teaspoon hot chilli flakes
4 large eggs, beaten
salt and freshly ground black pepper
handful of parsley, leaves finely chopped and stalks discarded, to garnish

- **METHOD**

Heat the oil in a nonstick frying pan over a medium heat. Once hot, add the onion and green pepper and cook for 3–4 minutes until starting to soften. Add the cherry tomatoes and cook for a further 2–3 minutes, then stir in the Turkish red pepper paste, pul biber, paprika and chilli flakes, along with a splash of water.

Cook for 1–2 minutes until fragrant, then pour in the eggs and season with salt and pepper. Stir for 3–4 minutes or until the eggs are just set. Garnish with the chopped parsley to serve.

DIPPING SUGGESTION
Turkish bread or toast.

Ssamjang

Ssamjang is really popular as a side dish on a typical Korean barbecue table and the ingredients can be found at Asian grocery shops. I love to serve it with grilled meats like pork or chicken, alongside lettuce cups and lots of *banchan* (Korean pickles). If you're making it for a big gathering, simply increase the quantities.

- SERVES 2–4

4 tablespoons doenjang
2 tablespoons gochujang paste
2 teaspoons granulated sugar or maple syrup
2 garlic cloves, crushed or finely chopped
4 spring onions, finely chopped
2 tablespoons sesame seeds
2 tablespoons sesame oil
4 teaspoons rice vinegar
salt (optional)

- METHOD

Add everything to a mixing bowl and stir to combine. Taste for flavouring and add a little more gochujang for extra heat, rice vinegar for sourness and salt if needed.

DIPPING SUGGESTION
Grilled meat and lettuce cups.

Spicy Garlic & Sun-Dried Tomato Prawns

This dip is inspired by *gambas pil pil*, a famous Spanish prawn dish, with the addition of sun-dried tomatoes.

- SERVES 4

100 ml (3½ fl oz) olive oil
6 garlic cloves, finely sliced
3 tablespoons sun-dried tomatoes, roughly chopped
1 teaspoon chilli flakes
325 g (11 oz) raw king prawns, peeled
1 tablespoon sherry vinegar
handful of parsley, leaves finely chopped and stalks discarded
salt and freshly ground black pepper

- METHOD

Heat the olive oil in a wide frying pan or casserole dish over a medium-low heat. Once hot, add the garlic and cook for 6–8 minutes until fragrant and softened.

Add the sun-dried tomatoes and chilli flakes, and cook for a further minute before adding the prawns, along with a pinch of salt. Cook for 3–4 minutes, or until the prawns turn pink, then remove from the heat.

Stir in the sherry vinegar and the parsley, and finish with a generous grind of black pepper.

DIPPING SUGGESTION
Crusty bread.

Black Chickpea Hummus Bil Lahme

This makes a great dinner plate as everything's served on top of the hummus. Just grab your favourite bread and dip in.

- SERVES 4

2 × 400 g (13 oz) cans black chickpeas (kala chana)
2 tablespoons tahini
2 tablespoons lemon juice
1–2 garlic cloves, crushed
3 ice cubes
2 tablespoons vegetable oil
1 onion, finely chopped
400 g (13 oz) minced lamb
1 tablespoon baharat
150 g (5 oz) cherry tomatoes, quartered
½ cucumber, finely chopped
150 g (5 oz) radishes, finely chopped
1 teaspoon sumac
large handful of parsley, leaves chopped and stalks discarded
salt

- METHOD

Add the chickpeas and their liquid to a saucepan and cook over a medium heat until just about to boil. Remove from the heat and set aside to cool.

Using a slotted spoon, scoop the cooled chickpeas out of the liquid and place in a high-speed blender. Add the tahini, lemon juice and garlic. Add 200 ml (7 fl oz) of the chickpea water too, then blend until smooth, adding more liquid if needed. Add 3 ice cubes and season with salt, blend once more, then divide between 4 plates.

Heat the vegetable oil in a frying pan over a medium heat. Once hot, add the chopped onion, along with a pinch of salt, and cook for 3–4 minutes until starting to soften. Increase the heat to high and add the minced lamb and baharat, stirring to break up the lamb. Cook for 8–10 minutes until the lamb is cooked through and crispy.

In a bowl, mix together the cherry tomatoes, cucumber, radishes and sumac, and season with a pinch of salt. Divide the baharat lamb between the plates, piling it on top of the hummus, and top with the tomato and sumac salad. Scatter over the parsley to serve.

DIPPING SUGGESTION
Middle Eastern-style flatbreads.

Nam Jim Jaew

This spicy, sweet and sour Thai dip is so addictive you can have it with most things, but the classic way to serve it is to dip sliced steak into the *nam jim jaew*, then wrap it in lettuce and enjoy.

- SERVES 4

2 tablespoons jasmine rice (uncooked)
2 banana shallots, peeled
2 garlic cloves, peeled
2–3 red chillies, ideally Thai bird's-eye chillies
20 g (¾ oz) fresh coriander, leaves and stalks roughly chopped
2–3 tablespoons soft light brown sugar
2 tablespoons tamarind paste
2 tablespoons fish sauce
juice of 3 limes
salt and freshly ground black pepper

- METHOD

Heat a nonstick frying pan over a medium heat and add the jasmine rice grains. Toast for 3–4 minutes until golden brown all over, then set aside to cool. Once cool, crush using a pestle and mortar (or spice grinder/high-speed blender) until the grains resemble sand.

If your mortar is large enough, add the shallots, garlic, chillies and coriander, and pound with the pestle to form a paste, then add the sugar, tamarind paste, fish sauce and lime juice and stir to combine. Alternatively, you can do this in a food processor. Taste for seasoning before serving, adjusting as needed.

DIPPING SUGGESTION
Grilled steak, lettuce and rice.

Spinach & 'Nduja Cannellini Beans

This is great for lunch, comforting but healthy-ish!

- SERVES 2

2 tablespoons salted butter
1 leek, finely sliced
3 garlic cloves, finely sliced
2 green chillies, finely chopped
1 teaspoon dried thyme
2 tablespoons plain flour
400 ml (14 fl oz) milk
100 g (3½ oz) baby spinach
2 × 400 g (13 oz) cans cannellini beans, drained
100 g (3½ oz) 'nduja
1 tablespoon baby capers
salt

- METHOD

Melt the butter in a wide nonstick frying pan over a medium heat. Once melted, add the leek, garlic and chillies. Season with a pinch of salt and cook for 4–5 minutes until softened.

Add the thyme and plain flour. Combine the milk and 100 ml (3½ fl oz) water in a jug, then slowly pour this milk-and-water mixture into the pan, stirring well to remove any lumps. Add the spinach and cannellini beans and cook for 4–5 minutes more, until the spinach has wilted and the butter beans are cooked.

Meanwhile, heat a separate small frying pan over a medium heat and add the 'nduja. Cook for 3–4 minutes, or until melted.

Stir the capers into the beans, then divide between 2 bowls. Drizzle the 'nduja over the top to serve.

DIPPING SUGGESTION
Crusty bread or crispbreads for extra crunch. Or just a spoon!

Desserts

These indulgent sweet dips are best enjoyed with a spoon. Mix and match and impress guests with a couple of dips as part of a wider dessert table.

Mango & Lychee Sago Pudding

If you find yourself in South Asian mango season (usually April–June), you've got to make this refreshing Asian dessert. If ripe mangoes are unavailable, then you can swap them for tinned, or add a bit more lychee syrup if using underripe mangoes. You can also mix this up by using other sweet soft fruits, like strawberries, pineapple or papaya.

- SERVES 4

50 g (2 oz) coconut flakes
100 g (3½ oz) tapioca pearls
200 ml (7 fl oz) coconut milk
handful of ice cubes
1 ripe mango, peeled, pitted and chopped into cubes
425 g (14 oz) can lychees, drained (syrup reserved) and roughly chopped

- METHOD

Toast the coconut flakes in a dry frying pan over a medium-low heat for 2–3 minutes, then set aside.

Half-fill a large, heavy-based saucepan with water, and bring to the boil over a medium heat. Once boiling, add your tapioca pearls. Boil for 10 minutes, then remove from the heat, cover the pan with a lid and leave to rest for 10 minutes. Next, strain the pearls through a sieve and wash them under cold running water until they are cool and separated. Tip into a mixing bowl.

Add the coconut milk and ice cubes to the bowl and give this a good mix. Stir in most of the chopped mango and lychees (holding back a handful of each to decorate). Then add 2 tablespoons of the lychee syrup and taste for sweetness, adding a little more if required.

Serve in small bowls, topped with the reserved chopped fruit and the toasted coconut flakes.

DIPPING SUGGESTION
With a spoon.

Mocha Mascarpone Mousse

This is the recipe to turn to when you've got last-minute guests coming over and don't have much time, but need to impress. It almost tastes like a cheat's tiramisu without the ladyfingers. Serve in whatever bowls or decorative glasses you have.

- SERVES 4

2 teaspoons instant coffee powder, plus extra to serve (optional)
250 g (8 oz) mascarpone
50 g (2 oz) chocolate hazelnut spread
4 maraschino cherries with stems, to decorate (optional)

- METHOD

In a small bowl, mix the instant coffee with 2 teaspoons hot water and stir until dissolved. Set aside to cool.

Add 200 g (7 oz) of the mascarpone to a mixing bowl with the chocolate hazelnut spread and stir until combined. Add the cooled coffee and stir again.

Divide the mocha mascarpone mousse between your serving bowls or glasses, then top with a dollop of the remaining mascarpone and a light dusting of extra instant coffee powder, if liked. I like to serve these with a maraschino cherry on top for a retro twist.

DIPPING SUGGESTION
With a spoon.

Firni with Rose & Pistachio

This dessert hails from Afghanistan, and is like a set custard without the eggs. The floral notes of the rosewater and saffron, along with the subtly spiced cardamom, make for a classic but wonderful pairing. The nuts are traditional and provide a nice crunch, but you can leave them out for guests with nut allergies.

- **SERVES 4**

3 tablespoons cornflour
300 ml (½ pint) whole milk
2 pinches of saffron threads
ice cube
100 ml (3½ fl oz) double cream
50 g (2 oz) caster sugar
5 cardamom pods, seeds finely crushed in a pestle and mortar, husks discarded
1 teaspoon rosewater
1 tablespoon finely chopped green pistachios (optional)
1 tablespoon finely chopped flaked almonds (optional)
salt

- **METHOD**

In a small bowl, mix the cornflour with 3 tablespoons of the milk and set aside. Add the saffron to another small bowl, place the ice cube on top and allow to melt.

Meanwhile, pour the remaining milk into a small saucepan, along with the double cream, sugar and crushed cardamom seeds, and place over a low heat. Just as the mixture starts to steam (before it boils), reduce the heat to a very low simmer and stir in the cornflour mixture. Stir until combined and continue to cook for 2–3 minutes, or until the mixture thickens, then remove from the heat.

Stir in the saffron mixture, along with the rosewater, then pour into 4 small heatproof glasses or cups and set aside to cool for 10 minutes. Transfer to the refrigerator and leave to set for at least 2 hours. Just before serving, top with the pistachios and almonds, if liked.

DIPPING SUGGESTION
With a spoon.

Whipped White Chocolate & Blueberry Cheesecake

This one's inspired by a white chocolate cheesecake served at a restaurant I love in London, but I've deconstructed it a bit. You could swap the white chocolate for milk or dark, but I'd then suggest swapping the blueberries for strawberries or raspberries.

- **SERVES 6**

100 g (3½ oz) white chocolate
100 g (3½ oz) blueberries
1 tablespoon soft light brown sugar
100 ml (3½ fl oz) double cream
165 g (5¾ oz) cream cheese

- **METHOD**

Add the white chocolate to a bowl that fits snugly over a saucepan of simmering water (without actually touching the water). Stir until the white chocolate has melted, then set aside to cool slightly.

Combine the blueberries and sugar in a small saucepan over a medium–high heat and cook for 3–4 minutes, or until the blueberries are softened and about to burst. Remove from the heat and set aside to cool completely.

In a large bowl, whip the double cream until stiff peaks form.

In another bowl, combine the melted white chocolate with the cream cheese and mix until well combined. Gently fold in the whipped double cream.

Layer the whipped white chocolate cream mixture with the blueberry compote in your serving cups or glasses and enjoy.

DIPPING SUGGESTION
Your favourite biscuits.

Browned Butter, Chocolate & Ginger Cookie Dip

Cookie dough needs little explanation, but here I wanted to make a hot version that you can eat with a spoon. The nuttiness of the brown butter and hazelnuts pairs well with the dark chocolate and sweet heat from the crystallized ginger.

- **SERVES 2**

50 g (2 oz) unsalted butter
50 g (2 oz) caster sugar
25 g (1 oz) soft dark brown sugar
3 tablespoons milk
1 teaspoon vanilla extract
100 g (3½ oz) self-raising flour
½ teaspoon bicarbonate of soda
½ teaspoon sea salt
50 g (2 oz) dark chocolate, chopped into small pieces
1 tablespoon chopped blanched hazelnuts
1 tablespoon chopped crystallized ginger

- **METHOD**

Heat a 20 cm (8 inch) nonstick ovenproof frying pan over a low heat. Once hot, add the butter and let it melt. Once melted, increase the heat to medium and let the butter brown for 4–5 minutes, until it's a dark biscuit colour. Carefully pour into a bowl and leave to cool. Keep the pan for later.

When the butter is cool, add it to a stand mixer (or use an electric hand whisk) with the sugars. Cream the butter and sugars together, then add the milk and vanilla extract. Add the flour, bicarbonate of soda, sea salt and mix well until combined. Stir in the chocolate, hazelnuts and ginger.

Transfer the cookie mixture into your frying pan, pressing it down until flat. Bake in a preheated oven, 180°C/160°C fan (350°F), Gas Mark 4, for 10 minutes, then remove from the oven and allow to cool for a few minutes before eating with a spoon!

DIPPING SUGGESTION
With a spoon.

Coconut, Strawberry & Rose Dip

This one may be in the desserts chapter, but you could definitely serve it at brunch. Swap the strawberries and rose for raspberries and vanilla if you like, but add a pinch of sugar if you do.

- SERVES 2

150 g (5 oz) strawberries, hulled
2 tablespoons rose syrup
200 ml (7 fl oz) coconut milk, chilled in the refrigerator overnight
handful of finely chopped pistachios, to decorate

- METHOD

Arrange the strawberries in a small baking dish and drizzle over the rose syrup. Bake in a preheated oven, 200°C/180°C fan (400°F), Gas Mark 6, for 8–10 minutes, or until the strawberries have softened but still hold their shape. Set aside to cool.

Meanwhile, add the coconut milk to a stand mixer and whip until soft peaks form. Alternatively, you can use an electric hand whisk.

Serve the whipped coconut dip topped with the strawberries, drizzling over any extra rose syrup from the dish. Top with finely chopped pistachios and enjoy with cinnamon toasts for dipping (see below).

DIPPING SUGGESTION

Cinnamon toasts: In a small bowl, mix 100 g (3½ oz) softened unsalted butter with 4 tablespoons soft light brown sugar and 1 teaspoon ground cinnamon. Spread this mixture over 2 slices of white bread, covering both sides of each slice. Heat a nonstick frying pan over a medium-low heat. Once hot, add the bread slices and cook for 3–4 minutes on each side, or until caramelized. Slice into dippers.

Banana & Peanut Butter Affogato

This cheat's banana ice cream is loaded with peanut butter and condensed milk, and works really well with a good strong espresso.

- SERVES 2

2 shots of espresso
4 bananas, peeled and frozen overnight
2 tablespoons crunchy peanut butter
2 tablespoons condensed milk
50 g (2 oz) dark chocolate, frozen overnight

- METHOD

Pour the freshly made espresso into 2 bowls or heatproof glasses.

Add the frozen bananas to a high-speed blender, along with the peanut butter and condensed milk, and blend until smooth (you may need to do this in batches). Once blended, place in a suitable container in the freezer for 10 minutes, then scoop the banana and peanut butter ice cream into your bowls on top of the espresso.

Using a vegetable peeler, peel the cold dark chocolate into curls and sprinkle over the ice cream. Serve quickly!

DIPPING SUGGESTION
Crunchy biscotti, or just with a spoon!

Shrikhand Parfait with Saffron Peaches & Almond Brittle

Shrikhand is a sweet dish made of hung yogurt/curd. It's found in Western India and is usually flavoured with saffron and cardamom. Here I've used the straining method to turn it into a layered parfait. If peaches aren't in season, you could use plums or even apples (but you'll need to peel these first).

- SERVES 2–3

100 ml (3½ fl oz) natural yogurt
50 g (2 oz) flaked almonds
200 g (7 oz) caster sugar
2 tablespoons unsalted butter
pinch of saffron threads
2 peaches, pitted and cut into thick slices
1 tablespoon soft light brown sugar

- METHOD

Line a fine sieve with a piece of muslin or a clean cloth and place it over a bowl. Add the natural yogurt and leave for 2–3 hours to strain and thicken.

Meanwhile, make your almond brittle. Line a baking sheet with nonstick baking paper and add the almonds in one even layer. Heat the caster sugar in a small nonstick frying pan over a medium-low heat. Let the sugar melt without stirring (you can gently shake the pan if needed). Once melted, increase the heat to high and, once the caramel is a medium-dark colour, immediately pour it over the almonds. Set aside to cool and set. Once set, break the brittle into small shards.

In a second small frying pan over a medium heat, melt the butter. Once melted, crumble in the saffron, then add the peach slices and brown sugar. Cook for 3–4 minutes, or until starting to soften and caramelize. Remove from the heat and allow to cool.

To serve your parfait, layer up the brittle pieces, yogurt and peaches in a serving dish and enjoy.

DIPPING SUGGESTION
With a spoon.

1

Mangonada with Kiwi

Mangonada is a drink typically found in Mexico, where it's served with a chamoy straw. Chamoy is a Mexican sauce made from tamarind and can be bought online. I wanted to turn it into more of a dessert dip, so have left some of the fruit chunky and added kiwifruit for extra flavour. Go heavier on the chamoy and Tajín if liked; the quantities are just guidelines!

- SERVES 4

3 ripe mangoes, peeled, pitted and cut into small chunks
handful of ice cubes
100 ml (3½ fl oz) chamoy sauce
2 kiwifruits, peeled and cut into chunks
5 teaspoons Tajín (Mexican spice mix)

- METHOD

Add 2 of the mangoes to a high-speed blender with the ice cubes and blend until smooth.

Take out 2 glasses and add 1 tablespoon of the chamoy sauce to the bottom of each one, followed by 2 tablespoons of the mango purée. Top with a few chopped mango and kiwifruit pieces, then add ½ teaspoon Tajín to each glass. Continue layering in this way, alternating between the chamoy sauce, mango purée, mango and kiwifruit pieces and Tajín, until everything is used up. Enjoy!

DIPPING SUGGESTION
With a spoon.

2

Brûléed Lemon, Maple & Cardamom Possets

This simple dessert is perfect for a summery lunch or garden party. If you don't have a blowtorch, you can skip this step and instead sprinkle the tops with crunchy demerara sugar.

- **SERVES 4**

4 lemons, halved lengthways
300 ml (½ pint) double cream
6 cardamom pods, crushed using a pestle and mortar
50 g (2 oz) maple syrup
4 tablespoons granulated sugar

- **METHOD**

Using a small sharp knife, carefully cut around the insides of each lemon, then use a spoon to scoop out the flesh. Transfer to a high-speed blender and blend to a pulp, then strain through a fine sieve into a jug. Measure out 100 ml (3½ fl oz) to use in this recipe, and store any extra in the refrigerator for up to 5 days. Keep the sieve and jug aside for later.

Add the double cream to a small saucepan with the crushed cardamom pods. Heat over a low heat until just about to boil, then take off the heat and stir in the maple syrup.

Add the measured lemon juice to the pan and stir until combined; you should feel the posset mixture thicken. Strain this mixture back through the fine sieve into the jug.

Arrange the empty lemon halves on a plate, then divide the posset mixture between them. Transfer to the refrigerator to set for at least 2 hours. Just before serving, scatter the top of each one with the sugar. Using a blowtorch, melt the sugar until it is golden. Allow the sugar to cool slightly and harden, then serve.

DIPPING SUGGESTION
Enjoy with a spoon, cracking the hardened sugar layer first!

Images overleaf ⟶

1

2

Glossary of UK/US Terms

INGREDIENTS

aubergine – eggplant
beetroot – beet
bicarbonate of soda – baking soda
butter beans – lima beans
caster sugar – superfine sugar
chickpeas – garbanzo beans
coriander – cilantro
cornflour – cornstarch
courgette – zucchini
double cream – heavy cream
king prawns – jumbo shrimp
minced – ground
pepper (red/green/yellow/orange) – bell pepper
plain flour – all-purpose flour
rocket – arugula
spring onion – scallion
sultanas – golden raisins
sweetcorn – corn
tomato purée – tomato paste

EQUIPMENT

baking paper – wax paper
frying pan – skillet
grill – broil/broiler
muslin - cheesecloth
sieve – fine mesh strainer
tin foil – aluminium foil

Index

Acknowledgements

Writing a book about dips is no small feat, trying to encompass various cuisines and diets whilst making sure they're all delicious. Great for me as I love eating dips! I feel really lucky to have had such a fantastic team who brought so much fun and creativity every day, I couldn't love the imagery we created any more and how fun that everyone's hands made an appearance!

Cara, your photography is beautiful but so is your energy, thanks to Hudson too for all your help (and the playlists!) – the process felt so collaborative so thank you. Max, your props are always stunning, but it felt extra special to have you on board as a friend too. Kristine, thanks for being my right hand in the kitchen – bringing the laughter everyday and to Lu for stepping in to help and being so positive!

Thanks to the team at Octopus. To Samhita for commissioning me and to Izzy for taking over – thanks both for all your support. To Scarlet, for being such a lovely editor to work with as we brought the book to life and to Yasia for the stunning design.

And finally to my family – thanks for encouraging me to leave the 'traditional work path' behind to pursue a passion I never knew I could turn into a job! Thanks for taking my calls at all hours of the day to help brainstorm random ingredients together and for always taking my glut of ingredients as my fridge overflowed.

To Anai, who (by choice or force) ate every single dip in this book. Thank you for always bringing me love and encouragement, washing many(!) dishes and always giving me feedback like a restaurant critic!

About the Author

Sonali Shah is a trained chef, food stylist and recipe writer with over eight years' experience in the industry. She fell into this world as a career change, having previously studied for a degree in politics and economics, and has since had a variety of freelance 'food jobs', including cooking for Hollywood actors on film sets, as a private chef, and developing recipes for various food brands and publications. She has styled for various magazines, a number of cookbooks and social media video campaigns as well as for film and TV dramas. Her heritage and love of travel deeply influence and inspire the way she cooks and eats.